By the same author.

The Prophecy in You
Stepping Into Greatness
The Feast of Booths
The Feast of Pentecost
The Feast of Passover
Taking the Gates of the City
The Foundations of Prophecy

Dedicated to the Lord whose prophesy to me to write this teaching have inspired these words.

Anger's House of Cards
Unmasking the Deception

Dr. Steven Rocco, D.D.

Calvary International Publishing Company
Cromwell, Connecticut 06416
2018

Preface

The contents of this book, *Anger's House of Cards*, is inspired by years of study in pastoral counseling throughout my 43+ years of ministry. It is wrapped in a continued series, **Emotions Less Spiritual,** in what I consider to be God's extended grace to the church and His unending mercy in our journey to become more like Christ.

It is my hope that this teaching enlightens every saint, church leader, and all who are pursuing a Christ-like walk in their ministries. I pray it bring clarification to His work on the cross, the coming of the Holy Spirit in your lives, and the salvation experience He graces to you by His Everlasting Covenant.

I have re-inserted chapter 9 from my book "Stepping Into Greatness" because this is a vital part of the healing process with issues of low self-esteem and anger.

Dr. Steven Rocco, D.D.
President
Calvary International School of Ministry and Theology
2018

CONTENTS

Introduction

In 1985, almost 11 years into my Christian walk, I had enough emotionally in my inability to cope with other Christians in church and my constant hurtful emotions. My frustrations turned to uncontrolled anger and the destruction of my personal relationships. It cost me my ministry and certainly my marriage. When I was feeling distraught or despondent toward life and the difficulties it brought to my situations, I used to lash out in uncontrolled anger to alleviate the pressure I was encountering. I did not care who was in my path at the time, they were getting a full blast of the vile I would spew. The fallout was not a concern at that moment. I could always ask forgiveness afterwards, fall on the grace of God, and fully expected that those I had apologized to would let us pick up our relationship where we left off before the outburst. I was deceived in thinking there would be no ramifications. My thinking was Christ died for me and as Christians we must forgive one another no matter what sin was committed.

After repeating this process for several years, it finally came to full fruition in my life. It unfolded in two ways. First, the damage had already been done in my personal relationships. My loved ones had enough of the tirades. It cost me intimacy in my marriage, a destruction of trust, and created a world of deception. Secondly, I was beginning to hate the behavior in myself. I didn't like it but more importantly I didn't know how to stop it. I lacked the knowledge of what was happening in me and I needed help in getting to that place where I could control this emotion of anger so as not to hurt anyone again.

I had been crying out to God to change me. I did not like the man I had become. I desired to be more Christ-like in my behavior. The Lord was at work in me and He never gave up on what He desired for me to become. In early 1985, I was led to a counseling session on low self-esteem and its crippling effect on our Christian walk and relationships. To this day I thank God for the revelation of the author of the book and for the counseling course he prepared. It changed my life through Christ and set me on a path of reconciliation and deliverance from the bondage of uncontrolled anger. The title of the book is "Healing for Damaged Emotions" by Dr. David Seamands.

Sitting in this class and beginning to see a light at the end of the tunnel was revelation to me and the mercy of God. I was starting to understand where this uncontrolled emotion was seated and why. I had not yet placed Jesus on the throne even after 11 years of salvation. He was my Savior, but I needed to make Him Lord.

I really did not believe I was loved by God. If you told me this at the time, I would have denied it vehemently. When I counsel today, and this subject is broached 9 out of 10 times I get the same response from the counselee; *OF COURSE, GOD LOVES ME!* **I had come to learn that at the core of all our dysfunctions is this one truth; our disbelief of God's love for us.** In many people's lives foundations of dysfunction have been laid for them to build upon. It is generational and gets passed on through the ages. It permeates every area of us in society. Our government is built upon it, our businesses are inundated with it, and our personal lives reflect it constantly.

A system of works

For me to grab hold of the dysfunction and to stop the emotional bleeding, I had to come to terms with destroying the foundation of works I had built before I came to the saving grace of Christ. In my counseling class for some destroying the foundation of dysfunction was immediate or within in months and for others, like myself, it would be years.

Dr. Seamands spoke of the scenarios we create for a system of works in relation to being loved. He spoke about some walking into a football arena to watch a game, but we were bothered every time the teams huddled for a play. We thought they were talking about us. **The constant it's all about ME factor.** In another scenario he makes us picture a ladder and God is sitting on the top rung. We are climbing the ladder to get to God but every time we reach the top rung God has moved up a few more rungs out of reach. **The constant I am never good enough factor.** These examples were just a few of the exercises he used to get the class to realize our life was built on a foundation of works and that love had to be earned.

Over the next few months, I began to take control of the thoughts in my mind using the word of God. For every negative thought I would surround it with Scripture. Such as, thought: You'll never be good enough. Scripture: "I can do all things through Him who strengthens me" Phil. 4:13. Thought: You'll never be a success in life. Scripture: "For I am confident of this very thing, that He who began a good work in you will perfect it until the day of Christ Jesus" Phil. 1:6. This process was a spiritual battle daily. It had to be repeated repetitiously until I got it completely in my spirit. It took months but the revelation of the truth of God's love finally made its mark. The fallout from this process was not necessarily a win/win scenario. I had lost my marriage, my family, and my ministry.

It is not this way for everyone. For those who have lost it all. God is in the recovery business. He is a God of second chances. He never stops working on restoration and reconciliation once repentance has been achieved. In the damaged I had done in my personal and ministry relationships not all involved were able to forgive. We cannot force reconciliation we can only hope and pray for it no matter how much forgiveness we ask. The heart of the unforgiver is a matter solely for the Lord.

Is asking forgiveness repentance?

The common mistake that most Christians make is thinking that asking for forgiveness puts them back in right relationship. I never realized the damage I had done until it was over. This issue for those I was in relationship with was not a matter of sinning once in this area. That could be forgiven and forgotten but when it became a repeated occurrence monthly, weekly, and daily at times the bonds of trust had been broken.

Saying we are sorry is one thing and seeking forgiveness is scriptural. The issue is repeated offenses. This is not repentance and that is what was needed. Repentance is a 180-degree turn. You were walking one way and now you are going in the complete opposite direction.

If we do not understand what is causing us to lose our tempers and declare WWIII on our situations, then we cannot bring resolution and true repentance to the life condition we have created. There is a root cause that must be dealt with. At the root of all dysfunctions is the belief that God does not love us.

"I" verses "I AM"

One afternoon I was in a counseling session and the counselor was discussing different scenarios from previous sessions we had together. When we got around to self-esteem I had no idea what was about to happen. I was told I was HIGH-MINDED. He told me high-mindedness masks low self-esteem. Finally, revelation! A light went on and it was as if the Lord opened a window in my mind directly from His throne and poured in this wealth of knowledge on self-esteem. My life to that point had reflected the "I" in me and not the "I AM" of the Lord.

The Scripture tells us we are His tabernacle. His glory dwells in us (see John 4). In Genesis 17 the Lord gives Abram His name and Abram becomes Abraham. Abram went from "I" to "I AM" in a moment. Part of any covenant relationship is an exchange of names. This is rabbinical teaching. When God dwells in us through our salvation, He imparts His name in us and He takes on our name to fulfill covenant promise. The "I AM" is manifested in us through the Holy Spirit. Our "I" becomes "I AM."

High-mindedness is always the "I" and it can never be the "I AM." We must die to ourselves for the "I AM" to truly become a part of us. Without this occurrence our esteem will always be ruled by SELF. Self can never satisfy the soul. It can never bring us into an everlasting peace and joy. Self is a whirlwind of emotions that always has a hunger and thirst for selfishness and ME first. Self is the "I" in you. "I AM" is the life of the Spirit of God in us. The "I AM" brings the fruit of the Spirit which is love and all that is written in Galatians 5:22-26. Be not boastful—High-minded—this is Paul's instruction to us (Gal. 5:26).

A path worth traveling

As the Lord had destroyed my foundation of works and replaced it with Him, I was always learning about His love for me. My gifts began to manifest, and my demeanor had changed in noticeable ways. In response to this happening I began to act on keeping my past in the past. I disposed of all my teaching materials and tapes before the transition in my spirit toward control over this emotion of anger. All those years spent teaching and preaching the Word didn't mean anything if there was still a taint of uncontrolled anger in my voice and materials. I was determined to make a clean break of it. I refused to continue to live a life of unforgiveness toward others and wrap myself in a judgmental spirit. God had set me free!

I can discuss all the parental underpinnings in my life and place blame in everyone else except where it truly belonged; myself. After all my parents were only doing what they were taught to do and repeated the process learned from their parents. I broke the generational curse. I was determined not to hand it down to my children. It would end with me!

In this book you will read what I have learned to set you free from this bondage of witchcraft and deceit. Make no mistake, uncontrolled anger comes from a witchcraft spirit and deliverance at times is needed. I will describe the rooms of secrecy that surround this emotion. I pray it helps you to become all that God has for you in Christ Jesus and that you break the chains of bondage that have held you so far. This book is about FREEDOM and LIBERTY in the Spirit of God.

Absent Father dominate Mother household

My reasoning for this caption absent father, dominate mother household had nothing to do with blame on parental duties when raising children. It does have to do with a spiritual condition that sets a tone in our lives about who God is and the misnomers of His attributes. My father was very much physically present in the home I was raised in. He just didn't take much interest in my life unless I got in his way. If I did get in his way it was usually for financial support not much else. If I wanted to know something about changes taking place in my body as a boy, teenager, or young adult I was directed to my mother. Since her background came from being raised in the home of an alcoholic father she was not much help. I had to learn things on the street and with my peers.

This kind of treatment and I am convinced it was without guile, was commonplace in my home. At the time, I was fine with it because I knew nothing else. My parents were fine with it because they did only what they knew and were taught by their parents.

It would be years later when sitting in the counseling seminar on damaged emotions that I learned fathers needed to be involved in every way in the rearing of their children. That means not just financially but emotionally and spiritually. **We get our image of God from our fathers.**

Why is it a witchcraft spirit?

In 1 Kings 21 we are exposed to the true spirit of witchcraft in the life of Ahab and Jezebel. Ahab is coveting his neighbor Naboth's vineyard. He makes an offer to purchase the vineyard but Naboth's understanding of the Law of Moses concerning inheritance denies his offer saying it would violate the Law. *"The Lord forbid me that I should give you the inheritance of my fathers"* 1 Kings 21:3. The result of this response put Ahab into a depressed mood and he went to his bedroom to sulk.

Jezebel his wife saw him sulking and asked him what the matter was. He reiterated to her Naboth's response to his proposal for the vineyard. Jezebel was not an Israelite. She did not take the Law of Moses to heart nor did she care what the consequences of disobedience to that Law would do to Naboth (loss of his salvation). *"Thus, no inheritance of the sons of Israel shall be transferred from tribe to tribe, for the sons of Israel shall each hold to the inheritance of the tribe of his fathers" Numbers 36:7.* She did not fear God. Instead she told Ahab because he is king over Israel he could have what he wanted.

Ahab understood the Law and knew Naboth to be correct in not selling out his inheritance. It would mean the judgment of God on their situation. Instead he was perfectly fine to let his non-Israelite wife do his nasty bidding. Jezebel was just as much subject to the Laws of Moses as was Ahab. The king knew this but justified in his mind that it would be better for him if Jezebel did the deed to secure him that land which he coveted over in his heart. *"You shall not covet your neighbor's house" Exodus 20:17.* Jezebel had a different idea. *"Jezebel his wife said to him (Ahab)...I will give you the vineyard of Naboth the Jezreelite" 1 Kings 21:7.* Ahab did not care that he was breaking two of the Ten Commandments. *"Thou shalt not bear false witness against your neighbor" Exodus 20:16.*

Jezebel purchased false testimony against Naboth by giving him a banquet in his honor and sitting the paid liars next to him to bear false witness and proclaim Naboth blasphemed God. A sin punishable by death under the Law.

The principle of an absent father applies to this Bible story. Ahab let his wife take responsibility for something that clearly was his. He was happy to pass off his patriarchal office to the matriarchal spirit of the house. This is the spirit of witchcraft. Witchcraft deceives men into abdication of their God given responsibilities. Witchcraft is a Jezebel spirit. When men refuse to take patriarchal responsibility the love of God becomes tainted in the life of those effected by its reproach. It sets in motion the deception that God does not love us and places us on a path of works adopting a false understanding that says within us **if I can be perfect I will be loved.** This is a lying witchcraft spirit.

Ahab's responsibility was to uphold the Law and honor the inheritance of Naboth. Instead he abdicated his office and allowed his wife to seek false witness against him and plot his death. In doing so, Ahab faced the judgment of God through the prophet Elijah.

Perfectionism and our secret chambers

The spirit of perfectionism can be defeated through a constant barrage of the Word of God in our lives. Letting His Word inundate you and permeate your very being will give you the tools, weapons, and authority needed to overcome the negative battle you have been facing most of your life. It's a battle but Jesus has won it at the cross. His resurrection has conquered the death we face daily. The battle of our mind has been won and we have become overcomers. The word the Gospel of John uses in the Greek is *Nakia'*. It is more than the meaning of an overcomer. It says we are conquerors.

Perfectionism is a system of works that takes as its partners high-mindedness, low self-esteem, and deception. There are secret chambers of witchcraft ruled by the spirit of Jezebel in each of these partners of perfectionism. High-mindedness houses lie within its rooms egotistical actions, narcistic behavior, and a bragging spirit. Low self-esteem has depression, pornography leading to other sexual tendencies such as adultery, homosexuality, and spousal abuse accompanied by sometimes violence, always emotional abuse, and a spirit of control. Deception is the foundation to the other two. It administrates a lying spirit that lays a foundation built on a house of cards. When all these factors are put into play in a person's life you have **the perfect storm, uncontrolled anger.**

There is hope in God's healing power

The light at the end of this tunnel, our healing, sits in the power of the cross through the covenant promise of the Spirit of the Living God. *"Who pardons all your iniquities, who heals all your diseases; who redeems your life from the pit, who crowns you with lovingkindness and compassion..."* Psalm 103:3-4. The scripture in Psalms tells us He has forgiven our sins and heals us. He has renewed our lives from the continuous struggle in our minds and in our thoughts. He does not end there. Healing and deliverance for Him are not enough. He gives us authority (a crown represents authority and power) and the power to be overcomers, more than conquerors, with a robe of righteousness and mercy. He is empathetic to our cause.

In humility He cloaks us. In grace He adorns us. In glory He anoints us. In mercy He reigns in us. Our victory over uncontrolled anger sits in John the Baptist's confession, *"He must increase, but I must decrease" John 3:30.* The more we allow Jesus by His Holy Spirit to rule and reign in our lives, dying to ourselves and our selfish ambitions, the greater the life of Christ by the Holy Spirit will be present in us. We will produce the fruit of the Spirit spoken of in Galatians 5:22-25.

Identify and take captive

Our victory to overcome our uncontrolled anger lies in being able to identify when the volcano will blow. We need to set rules in place that are practiced and held to a strict regimen. We cannot do this alone. In this situation we will need to set those rules for all parties involved. It is important for the participants to adhere to the rules set forth. These rules will help us to recognize when our lack of control is entering the situation and to be able to defuse it before it becomes the tornado no one wants to experience.

In the chapters ahead, I will explain what some of these rules should be and how to exercise them in your life. Setting your eyes on the things ahead and not looking behind to what once was a past of despair. The journey away from uncontrolled anger is both liberating and powerful. It will increase your anointing, allow you to hear deeper into the things of the Spirit, and manifest your gifting to greater levels of faith. Exploring the possibilities of how to control our anger and set our walk on a firm ground spiritually will give us the freedom God has ordained for our lives. FREEDOM and LIBERTY are the goals that will achieve a break in the chains of bondage from uncontrolled anger.

1

Anger's Unwanted Friends

Perfectionism, Guilt, and Debt-Collecting

Perfectionism — an endless striving to please a false god. There are six characteristics of this behavior that need to be understood and identified if healing is ever to take place in the life of the Christian. The purpose of this chapter is to help you understand the grace of God at work and His lovingkindness toward you. In this process a day-by-day trust must be established so that you will come to the realization that we serve a loving and caring heavenly Father.

Six Perfectionist Characteristics

- *Ought To (I must)* — this is the actions of never doing enough or being good enough. The mantra of this characteristic is "should have," "could have," "if only."
- *Self-depreciation (I can't)* — low self-esteem that sets the tone of never being good enough combines with self-depreciation. You are not pleased with yourself therefore God is not pleased with you either. There is a constant striving in you to meet higher and stricter demands.
- *Anxiety (I fear)* — never feeling you will reach your

goals, always strapped with guilt feelings, blaming yourself, and sitting in condemnation from God while disillusionment cripples you.

- *Legalism (I do/I don't)* – Constant sensitivity to other people's opinions. To please others and God the legalist becomes trapped in guilt and anxiety on a false path to pleasing God. An adherence to rules and regulations intensifies the guilt and anxiety.
- *Anger (I burn)* – the building resentment toward yourself, others, and God. Dr. David Seamands, "Healing for Damaged Emotions" describes it this way, "This resentment is a caricature of a god who is never satisfied. A god whom he can never please no matter how hard he tries, no matter what he gives up or holds on to."
- *Denial (Not me!)* – refusing to confront our anger. Mood swings cause a duality in you. You're one person one day and another the next.

The grace of God is the foundational healing ointment for perfectionism. We need a daily dose of this Godly attribute to reprogram our thoughts and break the habitual negativity that is permeating the life of a perfectionist.

In every characteristic there is an imbalance that fluctuates in the life of the perfectionist. The perfectionist can be all these characteristics at one time creating the perfect storm that is experienced by everyone around them. Its outlying dominate characteristic is uncontrolled anger. Understand that a certain amount of these qualities is normal and necessary but, in the perfectionist, they are out of balance. There is only one ultimate cure for perfectionism and it is as profound and as simple as the *grace* of God. Grace operates not only as a means of salvation, but through our whole

Christian experience.

A reprogramming is needed in the life of the perfectionist because they are unable to come to an understanding of the grace of God and His love for them. This reprogramming is what Paul writes in *Romans 12:1-2*, *"Therefore I urge you, brethren, by the mercies of God, to present your bodies a living and holy sacrifice, acceptable to God, which is our spiritual service of worship. And do not be conformed to this world, but be transformed by **the renewing of your mind,** so that you may prove what the will of God is, that which is good and acceptable and perfect."*

The Greek word for renewing of the mind comes from a transformation within. The word is *metamorphoo*, to be transfigured by a supernatural change. The perfectionist cannot renew their mind without the indwelling power of the Holy Spirit. It is the life of God in us that makes the transformation. *"I have been crucified with Christ; and **it is no longer I who live, but Christ lives in me;** and the life which I live in the flesh I live by faith in the Son of God, who loved me and gave Himself up for me" Galatians 2:20.* This statement from the letter to the Galatians is liberating to those who are tormented by a spirit of perfectionism. The Holy Spirit is in them. If they continue to give way to the flesh, they will never realize this liberating fact. Denying the flesh and the systems of the world is key in seeing the chains of perfectionist bondage broken. To be set free from perfectionism you need to be heavenly minded.

The perfect will of God

There are six properties that constitute *the acceptable and perfect will of God* (Romans 12:2). The word perfect in this scripture is wrapped in God's never-ending grace. It has already been accomplished at the cross of Jesus Christ and resting in Him through the Holy Spirit makes this transition liberating to the soul. The perfectionist has wrapped their thought process in the world's system of works. No mistakes acceptable. God's grace allows mistakes and gives second chances. This is a huge difference and changes the way a Christian should think and act. It is out of the motivation of grace that we are free.

- Present your bodies a living sacrifice (1 Cor. 3:16-17).
- Make your body holy unto Him (2 Cor. 7:1).
- Make yourself acceptable to God (Romans 12:1).
- Render unto Him your reasonable service (Romans 12:1).
- Be not conformed to the world (Romans 12:2).
- Be transformed from the world (Romans 12:2).

The Greek word for perfect in Romans 12:2 is *teleios*. It means that which has reached its end. In other words, there is no more that needs to be done to complete it. The perfectionist needs to transition from a life of *"I can't make any mistakes or if I do, I just don't measure up"* to *"God has done it for me. I can rest in Him. His love for me will never change."* Those who walk in a perfectionist frame of mind must come to the realization THAT GOD'S LOVE FOR YOU IS NOT BASED ON WHAT YOU DO BUT IT IS BASED ON WHO HE HAS MADE YOU. This fact is wrapped in the ministry of Jesus Christ at the cross, His resurrection to overcome death, and the giving of the Holy Spirit of Promise at the Day of Pentecost. The Lord has done the work, perfectly, now we need to walk in His grace.

Many people cannot follow through on God's gracious love (*agapeo*-unconditional; no works needed). A reprogramming in these cases is needed. The parents of a perfectionist have placed unattainable goals in their lives. In most cases parents are living exponentially through their children to make up for what they themselves could not obtain in their childhood. These unrealistic expectations, impossible performance goals, conditional love and a subtle theology of works have crippled the mind of the perfectionist and set them on a path of unattainable works. It's a vicious cycle that must be broken before a foundation of grace can be set in its place. In most cases, the whole structure must be demolished before a new foundation can be set in place. This demolition is the love of God bringing the perfectionist to a place where they have nowhere else to turn except to the cross. It is at the cross that the perfectionist will obtain a "renewing of the mind."

"When every experience or interpersonal relationship from childhood to adulthood contradicts grace and love, it is very difficult to believe it and feel it." – Dr. David Seamands, "Healing for Damaged Emotions."

The perfectionist continuously has cycles of tears, repentance, salvation, and renewed promises. The promises generally tend to fade away. In some cases, the healing will come slowly. There are exercises that are important in the healing process of a perfectionist as follows;

- *Counseling therapy* — it is important to have an impartial party with counseling experience give an objective view on how to handle issues of perfectionism.
- *Journaling* — it brings healing to journal feelings that are weighing us down. It clears the mind and is a good therapy.
- *Reading* — good books are a proven therapeutic method in helping to alleviate perfectionist thinking.

- *Music* — the scripture tells us that worship ushers in the presence of God. Getting a worshipful spirit in us causes the negativity to flee.
- *God's Word* — there is no substitute for God's written Word. It is liberating and medicine to the soul. Memorizing the Word of God will give the perfectionist the weapons needed to battle the warfare raging in their minds.

There are times you will need to press home the importance of what you think and taking control over your thoughts and actions is a vital method for victory.

Getting His Word in your spirit

- *"We are destroying speculations and every lofty thing raised up against the knowledge of God, and we are **taking every thought captive** to the obedience of Christ"* 2 Corinthians 10:5.
- *"Finally, brethren, whatever is true, whatever is honorable, whatever is right, whatever is pure, whatever is lovely, whatever is of good repute, if there is any excellence and if anything is worthy of praise, **dwell on these things**"* Philippians 4:8.
- *"**Be anxious for nothing**, but in everything by prayer and supplication with thanksgiving let your requests be made known to God"* Philippians 4:6.
- *"And the peace of God, which surpasses all comprehension, **will guard your hearts and your minds in Christ Jesus**"* Philippians 4:7.
- *"**I can do all things** through Him who strengthens me"* Philippians 4:13.

Christians need to learn to trust God. Perfectionists are always trying on new yokes, which turn out to be burdens that cannot be carried.

> *"Take my yoke upon you and learn from Me, for I am gentle and humble in heart and YOU WILL FIND REST FOR YOUR SOULS. For My yoke is easy and My burden is light" Matthew 11:29-30.*

Christians must have an attitude of wanting all that God has for them. Christ's yoke is easy because it fits. We must remember the grace of God is operative not only in our salvation but in our entire Christian experience.

The evidence of His grace is prevalent throughout the Scriptures.

- The New Birth — Ephesians 2:8-9 and Romans 3:24.
- In our Life and Growth — Colossians 1:2, Hebrews 4:16, 1 Peter 3:7, and 2 Corinthians 12:9.
- Even in Death — 1 Peter 1:13 and 2 Thessalonians 2:16.

Healing our Perfectionism

The road to healing of perfectionism or any emotional problem is a process. There are no quick cures or magical formulas. We do need to consider that the process can be immediate by the supernatural move of the Holy Spirit. There is ample evidence in the Scriptures of Jesus bringing healing to emotional situations instantly. For most of us, it is a working out of our salvation as a process.

In many cases, our family roots may have caused some of our perfectionist tendencies. The importance of a good home life is aimed toward building sound emotional health and fostering true concepts of God. The process that brings this healing in our lives is to grow in grace. There are several ways in which the healing process unfolds.

- *The mind* – God desires to heal our distorted concepts.
- *Our feelings* – damaged emotions dictate our reactions to these feelings.
- *Our perceptions* – this is system of works that bases our need for love on what we do not who we are. We enter a put ourselves down emotionally. Never a satisfactory evaluation.
- *In relationships* – this is a walk of double mindedness. We are joyful one day and a nightmare the next.
- *Our memories* – the soul is the battleground between flesh and spirit. The perfectionist will never give themselves a break when it comes to past actions.

The graciousness of God corrects false concepts, calms tension, clears faulty views, soothes hurt feelings, and forgives past failures.

Much of our associative and cognitive understanding stems from two areas of our life; *unpleasable parents and unpredictable home situations.* Perfectionists are trained from an early age, setting in root causes, about imperfect acceptances that later in life manifest themselves in adulthood. This results in uncontrolled anger. It is a mechanism within us that vents our frustrations because no matter what is done there is no pleasing of parental authority or any authority.

A woman who scolds her daughter for getting her dress dirty teaches the girl to associate unrealistic demands from her mother with God's expectations. Children who grow up in alcoholic homes find unpleasable parents at every turn of their childhood especially if there is an explosive temper with the alcoholic or the parent who is dealing with an alcoholic spouse. Such home situations are the breeding grounds for emotional cripples and perfectionists. Unpleasable parents, unacceptable self, unrealistic expectations, unattainable standards, unclear signals, and unendurable conflicts all program children in the wrong direction with the wrong kind of responses.

At times, some children blame themselves for their parents' downfall in life. In 1987, I was pastoring a church in Granby, CT. I began to counsel a man in my church who had a consist addiction to cocaine. He had been to several rehab centers both Christian and secular. Nothing worked. His next stop was prison unless he entered a drug rehab center where I was the pastoral counselor. In many cases, it is not the obvious that needs to be healed but the hidden. We want to get the drug addict off the hard drugs but never deal with the emotional trauma that led them there. Secular rehab centers, although they have their worth, do not have the knowledge to counsel their clients in matters of the spirit. As I began meeting with him, the Spirit of God led me to ask some probing questions about his mom and her relationship with him. The more I probed, the angrier he became until finally God surrounded Him with His love and grace and a well of tears flowed from him. He believed he was the cause of her nervous breakdown. He couldn't deal with it and tried to bury his hurts in the cocaine drug scene. He took on the blame for his mom and felt he needed to punish himself. Cocaine made him forget even if just for a moment. In this case scenario, the underlying factor was low self-esteem. The more he did the coke the deeper he dug his emotional pit. This led him to a crossroad where he had to decide, the path of cocaine or change paths and seek true healing. He chose the latter. Through solid Christian principles and emotional healing, I was able to show him why he was not responsible for his mother's illness.

Healing is a process. It touches various levels of a person's life. God's grace works on various areas of our lives. God applies positive assurances of hope and help through His grace, as one works through causes that have inhibited growth and freedom. The power of God's grace plays an important role in beginning and sustaining the process. When grace is applied to the two primary causes of emotional disorders, *unpleasable parents and unpredictable home situations,* the process results in changed lives, prosperity and spiritual promotion, and growth by maturity. The result is we become more like Christ in every aspect of our walk. Our responses to situations that were once an ignitor for our damaged emotions, particularly uncontrolled anger, have now become a Christ-like reaction encompassed in God's grace.

Anger and resentment

The anger and resentment that is usually built up in the perfectionist stems from feelings of injustice. The common theme among them is their irrational thinking that they didn't ask to be brought into the world. Their cry is they didn't choose their parents, their siblings, or their circumstances. The cry is a plea to set the world straight according to their feelings.

The cure for these feelings is the cross of Christ. On the cross Jesus experienced all the injustices that could have been heaped upon anyone person. He took our injustices on Himself. He understands the feelings of our infirmities. His work on the cross reconciled man to God. By faith in Him and His work on the cross, we can find reconciliation and peace. We no longer need to be perfect ourselves or perfect the imperfect and unjust world around us. We can put our trust in His perfect work.

Super You and Real You

Perfectionists need to learn to distinguish between the 'Super You' and 'Real You' in their lives. They need to be honest about which one they present to God and to others. It is important that they learn to abandon the masquerade of the 'Super You' and express themselves in the 'Real You' of everyday relationships. If they will work toward filling the void and emptiness of their lives by the gift of God's grace through Jesus Christ.

Certain basic needs are not met in the perfectionist's life. They have been denied feelings of security, acceptance, belonging, value, and worthiness. Instead an invasion of developed anxiety, feelings of insecurity, feeling unloved, and unworthiness set in. Becoming born-again does not wipe out these feelings of inaccuracy. It is only the beginning of the process on the road to recovery. When a person becomes a Christian, why don't all the negative aspects of their life disappear? The New Testament clearly assumes that growth in grace toward freedom from sin is a process in every Christian's life. *"...work out your salvation with fear and trembling"* Philippians 2:12. We don't become perfect when we receive Christ; we begin the process of growing up into "mature manhood" (Ephesians 4:13).

The Super You is a false idealized image of what you think you must be. It puts demands on you to live up to what you are not. It denies your legitimate emotions that need fair and proper expression. Anger is always seen as sinful, contrary to what Scripture teaches. Conflict is always seen as self-caused. Our Super You distorts the meaning of being happy and it stifles real joy.

There are no good feelings or bad feelings. There are emotions that are sinful or righteous until we act on them.

How you handle emotions determines whether they lead to righteousness or sinfulness. The three most misunderstood and clouded emotions in the souls of men are *anger, conflict,* and *happiness.*

- *Anger* – why is anger considered to always be sinful by some people? How can anger be expressed and not be sin? (see Ephesians 4:26 and John 2:13-17). Jesus expressed anger yet never sinned.

How does the suppression of legitimate anger work against a person? Properly controlled anger is a God-given emotion. It is when we show excessive anger that this action turns emotion into a state of sinfulness. This excessiveness turns the act of anger into resentment.

"Anger is a divinely implanted emotion; it is part of God's image in the human personality, and it is designed to be used for constructive purposes." – Dr. David Seamands, "Healing for Damaged Emotions."

Within the life of the perfectionist, their 'Real You' and their 'Self You' are constantly in conflict.

- *Conflict* – Why do some people believe they ought to get along with everybody? How does their 'Super You' get involved? Paul and Barnabas conflicted with one another over the attendance of John Mark during their evangelical campaigns. The disagreement separated their ministries, but they did not sin (Acts 15:37-39).
- *Happiness* – Do you always have to be happy? Are Spirit-filled Christians ever depressed? When examining these two questions we must understand that there is a difference between emotions and will.

Why is it okay to express all kinds of feelings such as grief, sorrow, hurt, loneliness, struggle, and even depression? What can be done to free and unmask our 'Real You'? When you stop wasting your spiritual energies maintaining this false 'Super You', and start using those energies in cooperating with the Holy Spirit for true growth, you will find yourself free in Jesus Christ, liberated from false oughts, and shoulds, freed from the approval and disapproval of other people, freed from the awful condemnation of the performance gap between what you're trying to be and what you really are.

Depression

It is important to understand that depression is not necessarily spiritual failure, and that it attacks even the greatest of saints. There is a distinction between guilt-caused depression and depression resulting from temperament. We need to learn to accept our temperaments, see ourselves as we are, and praise God for all we experience.

In 1 Kings 19:1-5 Elijah had just called down fire from heaven and the prophets of Baal were defeated. Queen Jezebel heard what Elijah had done and swore an oath to kill him. When Elijah heard what Jezebel had sworn to do he went and sat on a hill under a Juniper tree and asked the Lord to take his life (v4). He was depressed but he did not sin. These depressions do not seem to be related to spiritual problems, but to circumstances that created tension and anxiety. When anybody, including prophets and saints, faces strenuous emotional crises and decisions, the human personality experiences a certain degree of depression and anxiety. It is normal to have these feelings.

There is a distinction between guilt-produced depression and depression which results from the temperament of a person. The following is a general principle to define depression caused by sin and guilt. A concrete, specific feeling of guilt which can be related to a, precise act or attitude is generally a true and reliable feeling of guilt. And the emotions that follow can be real guilt and real depression for a real transgression.

On the other hand, a vague, all-inclusive umbrella of systematic self-accusation, general, overall feelings of anxiety and condemnation which cannot be pinpointed—these are generally signs of pseudo-guilt and just plain depression that have come from emotional sources.

When we look at depression, and how it expresses itself in individual temperaments, we must allow for the differences. Two married people need to understand each other's temperament and allow the other to function, without attributing behavior caused by temperament to a spiritual problem. Also, the person whose temperament is easily depressible must learn how to accept themselves as they are. Self-recrimination and guilt can create a more serious depression.

What confuses many Christians is that both our natural temperament, and the supernatural (our spiritual lives), our feelings and our faith, operate through the same equipment, much like a combination Smart TV, iPhone, and iTunes all in one console. Satan tries to confuse the two and turn our temperamental depression into spiritual depression, and ultimately to defeat us and break us down.

When we become born-again we still must operate in the flesh we were born with in the natural. Even though our new nature is heaven sent we must still contend with the temptations of this world we live in. The only difference as penned by Oswald Chambers, saying that the new birth, instills in us "the disposition of Jesus Christ." The fact that you have become a Christian does not mean that from now on you cease to live with yourself as yourself. Paul was still very much Paul after his conversion. Yet consider Paul's statement, *"We have this treasure in earthen vessels" 2 Corinthians 4:7*. Paul was quite aware of both the natural and the supernatural working within the Christian personality.

Satan tries to turn temperamental depression into spiritual depression and carry the natural mood of depression into a state of spiritual defeat, doubt, and despondency. The key to understanding depression is to learn to accept your personality and acknowledge your temperament. Our personality is that equipment God has given us; it is all we have. We are earthen vessels. We have infirmities that continually beset us. The Spirit however helps us in our infirmities. He takes up the slack that in our own persons we can't provide. We must learn through faith how to let Him work to control more of our feelings and not let Satan use these feelings to produce defeat and despair. But consider *Philippians 4:4-7, "Rejoice in the Lord always; again, I will say, rejoice! Let your gentle spirit be known to all men. The Lord is near. Be anxious for nothing, but in everything by prayer and supplication with thanksgiving let your requests be made known to God. And the peace of God, which surpasses all comprehension, will guard your hearts and your minds in Christ Jesus."*

Dealing with Depression

There are times and occasions when depression may stem from physical causes. The manifestation of this may result in issues of uncontrolled anger. We need to learn how to deal with depression-producing anger and to grasp some of the practical and positive things that can be done to handle depression while it is occurring. There are reaction patterns that lead to depression.

- *Indecision* – the depressed person feels trapped with no way out. They are afraid to say no out of fear of hurting someone. They are procrastinators because they want to avoid risk. This kind of indecision often precedes depression.
- *Anger* – depression has been defined as *'frozen rage.'* Anger that seethes or simmers almost surely cause depression.
- *Injustice* – a sense of justice is good; but out of balance and mixed with anger, it produces depression and bad relationships.

There are practical decisions that can be made if we would only take the initiative. People suffering from depression often just sit there and conform to every shape they are forced into. They respond in the same old self-hurting ways they fell into in their childhood.

- *Avoid being alone* – as hard as a problem may be, withdrawal only isolates a person further from reality and truth.
- *Seek help from others* – people who generate joy and who are positive about life can help focus on love of life. It is very hard to come out of depression without the help of concerned people.
- *Sing! Make music* – music is an ancient cure for depressed moods (1 Sam. 16:14-23). The Apostle Paul sang (Acts 16:25) in difficult places and encouraged Christians to use songs and melodies (Col. 3:16).
- *Praise and give thanks* – the key is to remember the simple things of everyday life. The biblical command is

to be thankful, not necessarily to feel thankful. God promises His peace to those who do this (Phil. 4:6-7).

- *Lean on God's Word* – especially the psalms which express feelings that correspond with depressive emotions. There are 48 psalms that speak to this condition. Reading these psalms aloud helps reinforce the strength, comfort, and hope needed to soothe the depressed spirit.

- *Rest in the Holy Spirit's presence* – the psalms express hope in the presence of God and speak of the help (health) of His countenance (Ps. 42:5). God's nearness and presence can heal and calm. The indwelling Holy Spirit will comfort us (John 14:16).

As humans we have emotional, physical, and spiritual limitations. Pressing ourselves beyond our strengths causes disorder and malfunction. Depression itself may be a sign that we are pushing ourselves too hard or not treating our bodies properly. It is not the circumstances that cause depression but rather our reaction to those circumstances.

There are primary reactions that lead to depression; indecision, anger, and injustice. Perfectionists have a disproportionate sense of justice creating an imbalance in their thought process which ultimately leads to depression. The biblical story of Martha and Mary displays an acute sense of injustice in the emotions of Martha (see Luke 10:38-42). Martha's feelings were hurt that she was in the kitchen preparing the meal while her sister Mary sat at the feet of Christ. Martha felt an injustice was being done which led her to complain to the Lord about Mary's priorities. Jesus wasted no time in dealing with Martha's attitude and perception. In receiving this rebuke from Jesus Martha sought forgiveness.

The importance of forgiveness is critical in staving off depression. A lack of forgiveness can tremendously hurt relationships and destroy marriages, partnerships, and churches. Vengeance is a prerogative of the Lord and must remain with Him. *"Never take your won revenge, beloved, but leave room for the wrath of God, for it written, Vengeance is mine, I will repay, says the Lord. But if your enemy is hungry, feed him, and if he is thirsty, give him a drink; for in so doing you will heap burning coals on his head. Do not be overcome by evil but overcome evil with good" Romans 12:19-21.*

The Lord has a system of fair justice. A human's sense of justice is to take things in their own hands and cause more bitterness and grief. Forgiveness is a strong motivation in God's eyes. He sent His Son to the cross for our sins. How can we hold a wrong against anyone when we are sinners ourselves? Our Christian lives must be reflected in no judgment zones wherever we may be. Love must be the motivating factor and forgiveness must be wrapped in God's love.

"But Jesus was saying, Father, forgive them; for they do not know what they are doing" Luke 23:34.

Guilt and Forgiveness

Sin produces guilt and our sense of guilt can lead to an overly sensitive conscience and a pressure of having to reach unreachable *ought to(s) or I must(s).*

Some Scriptures define the parameters of the *ought to or I must* syndrome by relating it to conscience. *Romans 2:14-15,*

"For when Gentiles who do not have the Law do instinctively the things of the Law, these, not having the Law, are a law to themselves, in that they show their work of the Law written in their hearts, their conscience bearing witness and their thoughts alternately accusing or else defending them..." and 1 Timothy 4:2, "...by means of the hypocrisy of liars seared in their own conscience as with a branding iron..."

There are two major causes of the emotional problems among Christians: (1) Failure to receive forgiveness and (2) Failure to give forgiveness. In many cases, it is difficult for Christians to accept God's forgiveness. Why do people insist on wanting to pay their own debts? Why do they feel they have to do more that God asks? In these scenarios the grace of God is too often forgotten or neglected. It has not penetrated to the level of our emotions, or into our interpersonal relationships. This failure to know and feel grace drives many Christians into a cycle of performance.

In Matthew 18:23-25, Jesus relates the parable of the servant who is forgiven his debt to the King and released from a life in debtors' prison until the debt could be repaid. Rejoicing in freedom he shows no mercy as was given to him when he seeks out a servant who owes him a debt. He immediately casts the servant into prison when he could not repay. His neighbors seeing this reported it to the King. The King recalls the servant to His court and rebukes him for not forgiving his brother when the King had mercifully forgiven him. The King then, throws the servant in prison.

In this parable, to some, the King seems harsh and unloving. But did the servant realize what the King had done for him in forgiving his debt? Why was the servant so hard on the one who owed him? At the onset of this parable, we may think this depicts God as unreasonable and overdemanding, since the unforgiving servant was put in jail. The parable reveals the mercy of God (18:27) which is also balanced by His justice. The truth is that God forgives unconditionally, but that forgiveness does not take effect until the forgiven person accepts forgiveness and becomes forgiving themselves (18:35).

"My heavenly Father will also do the same to you, if each of you does not forgive his brother from your heart" Matthew 18:35.

Forgiveness is at the epicenter of the Christian faith. It is the accomplishment and the right earned at the cross of Jesus Christ. The Lord is adamant in this very thing; forgiveness is the heart of the Living God. *"If we confess our sins, He is faithful and righteous to forgive us our sins and to cleanse us from all unrighteousness"* 1 John 1:9 and *"...little children, ...your sins have been forgiven you **for His name's sake**"* 1 John 1:12.

When Jesus taught us to pray in Matthew 6:9-13, The Lord's Prayer, He spoke of the only conditional terms in the prayer, *"...And forgive us our debts, as we also have forgiven our debtors..."* (v.12). When trying to understand forgiveness, we need to see that biblical principles are an important and essential ingredient for mature mental health. Our difficulty lies in the dynamics of our interpersonal human relationships. Our sense of justice, fairness, and fair play when demonstrated and exercised through an imbalance in our human nature and not controlled by the Spirit and God's eternal love, causes bitterness, resentment, and unforgiveness. These worldly emotions can set us on a course of destruction for years to come causing us to miss the blessings of God in our lives. We will not walk in the freedom and liberty He has given us. Our joy will never be made full in this life.

Forgiveness is basic and fundamental to God because Jesus paid the price. The Lord has made us for grace, acceptance, and love. The *ought to or I must* of our lives is built into us through our human emotions do to the fall of man. We have been programmed with a love through works mentality. Our only hope to break this cycle is a renewed mind that only comes through our regeneration; the cross of Jesus Christ and our acceptance of Him as Lord and Savior over us.

We are Debt-collectors

There is a crucial relationship between receiving forgiveness and giving it. The unforgiven are the unforgiving. It is this failure to forgive another that hinders and destroys so many relationships. If we have an unforgiving spirit, we cannot have fulfilled relationships. When we become debt-collectors we have entered a self-defeating activity. Debt-collectors never erase the memory tapes. They have downloaded every hurtful saying, disagreement, and wrong ever brought against them. It is in their memory banks to recall at a moment's notice to strike back at the heart of the ones they are in relationship with when needed. They use it to lift themselves above the ones they are in relationship with so that they have a sense of self-worth. This self-worth is built on a cracked foundation. Debt-collection is ruled by an unforgiving spirit guided by divination and witchcraft. It never brings reconciliation or forgiveness, but it most assuredly walks in division, unforgiveness, and revenge.

A debt-collector is not interested in sticking to the subject matter at hand when a disagreement arises. They want to justify why they are right at any cost. They will notoriously raise a past matter (hurtful, root cause never dealt with) when confronted with their own sin. This is a display of unforgiveness meaning they never placed the matter under the blood of Christ and are still holding a debt against the one who committed the offense. This occurs in all aspects of societal relationships, but it is most prevalent in marriage and in church related matters.

There are three ways to know whether we are still harboring unforgiveness toward someone. (1) Examine our attitude on resentment, (2) Examine our attitude on responsibility, and (3) Examine our attitude on reminders. Our attitudes reveal our hidden emotions on a debt we may have toward someone.

- *Examine our resentments* – Is there someone you are resenting or not letting off the hook?
- *Examine our responsibilities* – How much are you blaming others for the things you do?
- *Examine our reminders* – How can guilt by association hinder a person from being completely forgiven?

"Therefore, since we have a great high priest who has passed through the heavens, Jesus the Son of God, let us hold fast our confession. For we do not have a high priest who cannot sympathize with our weaknesses, but One who has been tempted in all things as we are, yet without sin. Therefore, let us draw near with confidence to the throne of grace, so that we may receive mercy and find grace to help in time of need." Hebrews 4:14-16.

2

Unmasking the Deception

High Mindedness, Low Self-Esteem, A Lying Spirit

It is true that the fundamental sin in our Christian walks is that we fearfully seek safety behind our masks of 'authority' and 'submission' rather than endeavor to meet God at the cross where He offers love and acceptance. The fundamental antidote for repairing our brokenness must be genuine repentance. We must allow God to renew our minds and root out the generational, emotional, physical, and spiritual hurts in our lives. Repentance involves admitting the sinfulness of our safe-seeking methods and embracing dependence on God and openness in our relationship to Him.

Identifying the problem

In the New Testament, the word infirmity has a more figurative use. The Greek word used for infirmity is a negative form of the word strength (*astheneia*), which means a want of strength, a lack of strength, a weakness, or a crippling. Infirmity rarely refers to a physical problem in the New Testament. It is more often a moral, mental, or emotional weakness. Infirmities are not sins; they are crippling weaknesses which help undermine our resistance to temptation. They make it more difficult for us to avoid sinning, and easier to fall into sin. Jesus bore our infirmities in the following ways;

- Desperation with life and depression (Matt. 26:37-38).
- Facing the pain of false accusations (Matt. 26:39-67).
- Being scoffed, mocked, and ridiculed (Isa. 53:2-3).
- Dealing with death and grief (Isa. 53:2-9).
- Inability to pray (Ps. 22:1).

The Old Testament describes infirmities through animal blood sacrifice made by the priests. They were to offer animals without blemish or infirmities. An infirmity was a physical defect in a man or animal. In infirm animal could not be sacrificed and an infirm man could not offer sacrifice. In comparison the New Testament unlike the Old Testament describes infirmities to be emotional, mental, or moral weaknesses not physical characteristics.

Jesus bore our sins on the cross of Calvary. In doing so, our only hope for healing from our infirmities is the acceptance of His work on the cross. Our only hope of victory or success in these areas of life is through Jesus Christ. Jesus feels and understands our infirmities because of His Incarnation, "God with us." The Incarnation speaks of mediation through Christ as the perfect deity. He united with human beings by taking on Himself all human sins, though He Himself was sinless. As Mediator, Jesus has become our High Priest who understands fully the feelings of our infirmities.

"Therefore, He had to be made like His brethren in all things, so that He might become a merciful and faithful high priest in things pertaining to God, to make propitiation for the sins of the people. For since He Himself was tempted in that which He has suffered, He is able to come to the aid of those who are tempted." Hebrews 2:17-18

Hebrews 4:16 says come boldly to the throne of grace. The Lord is open to the feelings we experience in life and in a nonjudgmental way.

Low Self-Esteem — Satan's Deadliest Weapon

The effects of this emotional trauma in a person causes unnecessary depression, thwarted goals, estranged relationships, and ineffective Christian service. This is a pit of despair that puts Christians on a roller coaster ride. A constant marching in a circle and never getting to the desired goal of freedom and liberty in Christ. It is constantly beating the drums of negativity saying, *"you're not good enough," "you'll never accomplish anything,"* and *"I've seen better."* Low self-esteem sucks the very wind of hope out of your sails.

This weapon of the enemy kills incentive and creates disharmony within and without. Feelings of inferiority, inadequacy, and low self-worth produce these following results which Satan uses to cause failure and defeat:

- *Paralyzing your potential* – trapping you into a world of works and constantly needing approval.
- *Destroying your dreams* – your hopes and aspirations which lead to normal and successful programs of life are tainted and blemished never reaching full potential.
- *Ruining your relationships* – Feelings of inferiority reflect on God who made all men. A low estimate of God's person sometimes follows from a low estimate of yourself. Holding a low opinion of yourself creates an obsessive concern with self and creates tension with others because of selfishness.
- *Sabotaging your Christian service* – Christians function as a body. When a person downgrades their own worth and their own gifts, they put more strain on the rest of

the body. The body of Christ and His church works best when all the members function to the fullest of their capabilities. God can show His power and ability only through Christians who use their God-given abilities and talents. To hide your talents hides the glory of God, for we are made in His image. To use our creative skills manifests God's glory, for He created us in His own image.

There ten main areas of low self-esteem that Dr. James Dobson, of Focus on the Family, has identified in the Christian life. Any three of these may be more dominant than the others.

- Absence of romantic love in your marriage.
- In-law conflicts.
- Low self-esteem.
- Problems with children.
- Financial difficulties.
- Loneliness, isolation, and boredom.
- Health Problems.
- Sexual problems in marriage.
- Fatigue and time pressure.
- Aging.

One test of low self-esteem is to stand in front of a mirror. If you begin to point to what is wrong with the image in front of you rather than the image *(Psalm 139, thou are wonderfully made)* God created, it is likely that low self-esteem is sitting on the throne of your heart. In relation to the feelings of low self-esteem consider these four points.

- *Paralyzing your potential* – In Matthew 25:14-30, the Parable of the Talents, the motivation of the man with one talent and his desire to hide it was inferiority, inadequacy, and fear. When we fall into the trap of comparing ourselves to someone else's accomplishments it affects our self-image. Our sensitivity to failure is based on a faulty foundation of seeking God's approval through our works. Yet, the spiritual truth is that we are approved and accepted by God because Jesus paid the ultimate sacrifice. Through His shed blood we have approval and entry to the throne of grace.

- *Destroying our dreams and visions* – dreams speak of the future, they warn of danger, and they promise hope. Dreaming is aspiring to better things. It is having hope that the future holds success. In Proverbs 29:18 the Hebrew word for vision is literally translated revelation. *"Where there is no <u>revelation (vision)</u>, the people are unrestrained."*

   Revelation is understanding. It is the epitome of "once you were in darkness but now behold you walk in the light."

   Revelation is seeing the truth. "I was blind, but now I see." We are given a direction and our capacity to accomplish that direction is in full anticipation and preparation for the Lord's indwelling power in us.

   Fear inhibits. This emotion is a debilitating factor in the lives of many Christians. It keeps us from reaching our dreams. It is the fear of what someone would say, fear of taking risks, fear of breaking traditions, and the fear of failure that holds us back.

- *Ruining your relationships* – this emotion can cripple your relationship with God. When we despise who we are we develop misconceptions about God. Denying yourself and staying humble does not diminish your worth or value as a Christian. Some of the most difficult people to get along with are those who do not like themselves. There is a relationship between liking oneself and liking others. If you hate yourself, you are likely to think little of others. We need to have a healthy self-image to have good interpersonal relationships.

When we have a low self-image, we put burdens on those around us. We put a strain on them to constantly make us feel adequate and good. We must build ourselves up in Christ so as not to become arrogant and prideful. Our self-image must be centered in a Christ-like life otherwise we can become ensnared by pride and arrogance.

- *Sabotaging your Christian service* – Christians are filled with self-effacing excuses about their ability to do something. They fear getting involved and it relates to their low self-esteem. At times, this fear is rooted in pride rather than humility. It is very often that God choses the weak, the despised, and the unknown to do and fulfill His work (1 Cor. 1:26-31).

God can show His power more easily through those who do not have outstanding natural ability. He used Moses who was afraid to speak publicly and the Apostle Paul who apparently had all kinds of physical disadvantages. Jesus' disciples were all "out of their field" when He chose them. God can work through us if we give Him what we have. He then can take it and mold it and use it successfully. We can do all things through Christ who strengthens us (Phil. 4:13).

"I can do all things through Him who strengthens me." Phil. 4:13

Repairing our self-image

How a person thinks about themselves largely determines what they will become. The key to changing emotional hurts and problems is to repair our self-image. The importance in this healing process is to be wanted, feel worthwhile, and to be competent.

It takes more than physical changes to change the personality. Personality changes are more likely when people can alter the picture they have of themselves. A personality face can be reconstructed if their self-image can be altered. Positive change can take place. Self-concepts can affect relationships to God, ourselves, and to others. Our self-image is a description of a whole system of pictures and feelings, images, and emotions we have put together about ourselves. The way we look at ourselves and feel about ourselves way down deep will determine what we will be and what we will become.

Dr. Morris Wagner, in his book, "The Sensation of Being Somebody" describes three parts of self-image:
1. *A sense of belongingness.*
2. *A sense of worth and being.*
3. *A sense of being competent (being able to cope with life).*

Our self-concept comes from four sources; the outer world, the inner world, Satan with all his evil sources, and God and His Word.

Bad self-images can hinder good personal relationships. Botox and reconstructive surgery are prevalent in many people's lives so that they can have a better self-image. Yet, this is no guarantee of a better outlook on life. The changing of skin and bone structure statistically does not make people happier. It is more important that people learn how to change their self-image from within. A bad self-image affects what a person will be.

"For as a man thinks within himself, so he is." Proverbs 23:7

Belongingness, worthwhileness, and competence

When does the sense of belonging begin? In 2004, I was pastoring in Bristol, CT. I was counseling a man in my church who had a spirit of suicide. He was in constant torment. He felt rejected, disowned, and had no sense of belonging even though he was married and had a family. He could not find any joy or peace of mind. As I began to probe into his background I noticed a common thread all throughout the sessions we had. He never trusted the love offered in his relationships whether it was his wife, his children, or any of his family. He had abandonment issues and no matter what anyone had done for him, he filled his life with rejection.

As I questioned him about his relationship with his parents, it was revealed that he was not wanted by his father from conception. His father did not visit the hospital at the time of his birth until three days after he was born. His mother was so despondent about it that in her anger she named him after his godfather instead of his father as discussed. The reason was because his godfather visited her on the day of his birth when his own father did not. The father was off galivanting with another woman. Even though he was their first child which should have been a time of anticipated excitement for the family and a defining moment for him. It was an unmitigated disaster of rejection, disapproval, and abandon. These feelings would determine the emotional path this man would follow into his adulthood.

Most Pediatric Advocates across America agree that a child can sense rejection in the womb. It can lead to difficulties in a woman's labor and birth as well as cause the child to be colic and irritable once born. It creates an emotional handicap in the child that fosters low self-esteem issues from the beginning. Since our image of God is transferred to us by our fathers any rejection from them will certainly lead us to believe that God has rejected us as well. This creates a vicious cycle of acceptance and love through works alone. Without Jesus Christ, grace will not play a part in this tragedy. The foundation being laid in the lives of those who have walked this way is one of uncontrolled anger, lust, and lying. The cornerstone of this foundation is deception.

The spiritual battle to overcome these feelings of low self-esteem will always occur in the mind. The believer must take every thought captive and replace them with the Word of God. The foundation of negative thoughts once seeded in our youth that are now manifesting their poisonous fruit in our adulthood must be battled with God's eternal Word of grace. Such imaginations like "you'll never amount to anything in life," and "I am sorry for the day you were born" must be flooded with God's word in our mind repetitively; *"I can do all things through Him who strengthens me"* Phil. 4:13, *"For I am confident of this very thing, that He who began a good work in you will perfect it until the day of Christ Jesus"* Phil. 1:6, and *"Brethren, I do not regard myself as having laid hold of it yet; but one thing I do: forgetting what lies behind and reaching forward to what lies ahead, I press on toward the goal for the prize of the upward call of God in Christ Jesus"* Phil. 3:13-14. Replacing negative words formulating in our mind with the Word of God for as long as it takes gives us the victory over these self-esteem issues.

There are many events that set off the negative side of anger and anger's companions in our lives if we do not have the capacity spiritually to have been delivered from the poison of this fruit. It manifests itself when some of the following occur in our lives.

- When we fail.
- When we are under pressure and stress.
- When we are criticized even constructively.
- When we have financial difficulties.
- When we are rejected.
- When our relationships are under scrutiny.
- And many more like what was stated above occurs.

When the feelings of failure, rejection, or depression set into the believer's psyche the temptation to sin magnifies itself immensely. The giving in to the temptation results in sinful acts that are played out through pornography, sexual immorality, alcohol, drugs, lying, stealing, masturbation, and all other fleshly desires.

Our victory lies in the Word of God through the power of the Holy Spirit. Understanding that our sin is covered in the blood of Christ and walking in the belief of His forgiveness surrounds us with His love. We become more than conquerors.

A lying spirit

A lying spirit is witchcraft! It is explained to us in Isaiah 14:14, *"I will ascend above the heights of the clouds; I will make myself like the Most High."* Lucifer proclaimed himself to be above God and to lift his throne above the heights of heaven. This spirit was transferred to our flesh in the Garden of Eden through manipulation and deception (the two comrades of lying). It is the epitome of a 'ME' mentality. Consider Paul's explanation in Galatians 5. *"For the flesh sets its desire against the Spirit, and the Spirit against the flesh; for these are in opposition to one another, so that you may not do the things that please you"* Gal. 5:17. Paul capitalizes the name Spirit in this passage. Its meaning is the Holy Spirit. In other words, our flesh is set in direct opposition to God. He goes on to say that giving into the flesh puts us under the Law. *"But if you are led by the Spirit* (Holy Spirit), *you are not under the Law"* Gal. 5:18. The Law has been set in place in Creation to judge the world, both temporal and spiritual, and mankind. It is the Law that draws us to Christ (Gal. 3:24). It is the work of Jesus Christ that sets us free from the judgment of the Law and seals us in the promise of the Holy Spirit. When we lie and walk in a lying spirit we are in judgment of the Law and an enemy to the manifest Spirit of God.

So, what is behind a lying spirit?

Low self-esteem entrenches itself so deep within the psyche of man that lying becomes second nature to his personality. It is engrossed in exaggerations and partial truths to build up the person's self-esteem in the eyes of his fellow man. The root cause of this emotional deception is the lack of true knowledge within their heart of God's absolute unconditional love. This condition is so dominant in the person who is engaged in such activities that the half-truths become absolute truth in their minds. They have surrendered to the deception that surrounds this activity because their need to be loved outweighs their desire for truth. It is a high-minded condition that masks their low self-esteem.

The aspects of these actions are set in a foundation of the flesh as described in Galatians 5. *"Now the deeds of the flesh are evident, which are: immorality, impurity, sensuality, idolatry,* **sorcery (witchcraft)**, *enmities, strife, jealousy,* **outbursts of anger**, *disputes, dissensions, factions, envyings, drunkenness, carousings, and things like these, of which I forewarn you just as I have forewarned you that those who practice such things shall not inherit the kingdom of God"* Gal. 5:19-21.

The resolution

Our identity must be wrapped in the life of the Holy Spirit. It is no longer we who live but Christ lives in us. *"I have been crucified* (the flesh) *with Christ; and it is no longer I who live, but Christ lives in me; and the life which I now live in the flesh I live by faith in the Son of God, who loved me, and delivered Himself up for me"* Gal. 2:20.

Therefore, our battle sits in heavenly places over the control of our mind. Continuing to place God's Word in us daily, moment by moment, will give us the victory we so desperately need. Love rejoices with the truth (1 Cor. 13:6). God's Word sets us free from the torment of deception and lies.

Steps to Recovery

- Admit to being powerless over this compulsive behavior. *"For I know that nothing good dwells in me, that is, in my flesh; for the wishing is present in me, but the doing of the good is not"* Romans 7:18.
- Believe that God's power is greater than ourselves and can bring us to restoration. *"For it is God who is at work*

in you, both to will and to work for His good pleasure" Phil. 2:13.

- Make the decision to surrender your will to the care of God. *"I urge you therefore, brethren, by the mercies of God, to present your bodies a living and holy sacrifice, acceptable to God, which is your spiritual service of worship"* Romans 12:1.
- Examine yourself. *"Let us examine and probe our ways and let us return to the Lord"* Lam. 3:20.
- Confess to God, to yourself, and to others the nature of your deception. *"Therefore, confess your sins to one another, and pray for one another, so that you may be healed…"* James 5:16.
- In humility ask for Him to remove these deficiencies. *"If we confess our sins, He is faithful and righteous to forgive us our sins and to cleanse us from all unrighteousness"* 1 John 1:9.
- Set things right with those we have harmed. *"If therefore you are presenting your offering at the altar, and there remember that your brother has something against you, leave your offering there before the altar, and go your way; first be reconciled to your brother, and then come and present our offering"* Matt. 5:23-24.
- Prayer and Meditation. *"Let the word of Christ richly dwell within you…"* Col. 3:16.

Christ desires to set you free from the addictions of the deception of low self-esteem. Our identity as a new creation is in Him and we should never let our past dictate our future. Let God set you free!

3

Anger begets Anger

"A fool always loses his temper, but a wise man holds it back" Proverbs 29:11.

Generational curses always set the tone for the way we deal with life. If they are not covered in the blood of Jesus Christ, they can fester in our fleshly nature and saved or unsaved it will not keep us from eventually exploding into an uncontrolled rage. Christ has come to save us from these devastating acts of the flesh.

Our father's inheritance...behind the steel wall.

Learned behavior sets the tone for a child's future. If the child is raised in an angry home, it will damage the child's self-esteem and teach them that dysfunction is an acceptable standard in life. It will also teach them that uncontrolled anger is an acceptable method of dealing with life's situations. Paul addressed this several times in the Scriptures. *"Fathers do not provoke your children to anger; but bring them up in the discipline and instruction of the Lord"* Eph. 6:4. And, *"Fathers, do not exasperate your children, that they may not lose heart"* Col. 3:21.

Cruel parents usually have bad children. Too many parents are guilty of punishment when dealing with childrearing. The Scripture tells us to discipline and give instruction which is significantly different than punishment. Punishment is a principle stemming from revenge, but correction is a principle of affectionate concern. The Christian principle behind the differences of punishment and correction is taken from the Greek word *'paideia'* or child training, education, discipline, and nurturing instruction. *"All Scripture is inspired by God and profitable for teaching, for reproof, for correction, for training in righteousness"* 2 Tim. 3:16. While punishment is taken from uncontrolled anger's position of exacting revenge on the victim.

The intention of Paul's discourse in Colossians 3:20, "...that they may not lose heart," is taken from the Greek word *athumeo*; a broken spirit. If we do not handle discipline in our children in a loving (*agapeo*—Godly love) manner we are setting them up to fail and instilling in them a foundation of love based on works not grace. Love acceptance through works is a sure formula for failure while Love acceptance based on unconditional grace orders a man's steps.

Our image of God and how the Lord ministers to us is exacted from our fathers. If we have an absent father (you can have a father who was home with you but is never involved therefore making him absent—emotionally), you will grow into believing that God is absent from your life when you need Him the most. If we come from a home without a father (single mother household) our image of God is more matriarchal when handling life's crises. The patriarchal motivation is removed. A Godly patriarchal influence is essential in establishing emotional and spiritual well-being in children. In most cases, these examples of an absence of the patriarch in children's lives will result in an angry adult. This is a vicious cycle that can only be broken through the blood of Christ, the cross experience, and the Word of God administering healing into the situation. Otherwise, the anger personality will prevail from generation to generation. A never-ending cycle of dysfunction, hurt, and deceit.

The Blame Game

When uncontrolled anger raises its ugly head and sinks its fangs into its next prey the weapon of choice is not so much the destructive path of the spewing of anger but rather the deference of blame. In an uncontrolled life of anger, the person displaying the rage in many cases will transfer the blame onto the one who they are unleashing their venom on. Such as, "It's your fault I'm angry," or "You made me do this," and even, "Nothing I ever do is good enough for you."

The person with an anger issue without counseling or revelation directly from the Holy Spirit will never take responsibility for their actions. They are always looking to transfer blame. The cure for uncontrolled anger begins with an admission to the problem and the accepting of responsibility.

So many times, I have counseled the victims of this sinful behavior only to find they have stayed in the situation because they were convinced they were the issue. This is exactly what the person with anger wants; to control, manipulate, and transfer blame to take the spotlight off themselves. All the while they are dying inside emotionally, and they are spiritually empty having cast themselves into a pit of despair. Most times, not realizing where they have brought themselves because their high-mindedness has masked their low self-esteem, so they believe it is the fault of everyone else around them and the world in general.

Projectionism

The lying spirit is notoriously at work in the life of the

person with uncontrolled anger. A significant part of the deception of this sin in the life of believer is the unconscious ability to project their lies onto others to avoid taking responsibility for their own short-comings.

The definition of projectionism as prescribed in psychological terms is the unconscious act of ascribing to others one's own ideas or impulses – Webster's New World Dictionary.

There is a three-fold failure in this pattern that is quickly developed in people with uncontrolled anger. The deception is in the lies they believe about themselves and their actions.

- **Failure in believing what God said about them.** *"Before I formed you in the womb I knew you, and before you were born I consecrated (had reverence for) you"* Jer. 1:5.
- **Failure to trust God's love.** *"For God so loved the world (YOU), that He gave His only begotten Son, that whoever believes in Him should not perish, but have eternal life"* John 3:16.
- **Failure to love the right way.** *"...not as a result of works..."* Eph. 2:9. We should not live and love according to what we do or what is done for us but rather because of who we are in Christ.

All the listed failures above are in direct relationship to the sinfulness of self-protection. The sin is not in the longing or desire of protection but rather in neglecting the belief of God's adequacy and intentions to show love and give protection. In their fallenness they are committed to getting their own needs met in their own way, rebelling against God's design for finding life in Him.

Verbal Outbursts

I recently counseled a minister of a large international ministry about some issues he was having in his marital relationship. His call was initially to lay blame of his outbursts of anger on his wife. She was, according to him, the blame for all their problems and he was trying to build a case against her so to defer any responsibility on himself. In having previously spoken to his wife I discovered that his outbursts were getting more frequent than they had been in the last two years. It was beginning to turn physical. He was grabbing her violently and throwing her to the ground all the while screaming that he wanted a divorce. Her desire was to reconcile their differences as God would require. On the other hand, he refused to accept any responsibility for his actions and faults in the relationship. He refused any further counsel. They are since separated, which I recommended for her safety, and he still has not sought a divorce even though he will not reconcile. She is his third wife and had a history of this same behavior with his other two marriages. His children have lost his respect, his parents are afraid of him, and he lies about the situation to his ministry partners by placing blame on his wife to save what is left of his ministry.

There are several sinful actions that reveal the dysfunction in this minister's life through his verbal outbursts. All actions have consequences, whether good or bad.

- **Not accepting responsibility.** This sin goes back to the Garden of Eden. *"And the man said, "The woman whom Thou gavest to be with me, she gave me from the tree and I ate""* Gen. 3:12.
- **Justification of sinful actions.** Saul used the same reasoning in 1 Samuel 15:10-19 when commanded by God to destroy all that the Amalekites had including

livestock, children, and spoils. *"Why then did you not obey the voice of the Lord but rushed upon the spoil and did what was evil in the sight of the Lord?"* 1 Samuel 15:19.

- **Lying about the truth.** *"There are six things the Lord hates, Yes, seven which are an abomination to Him: ...A false witness who utters lies, and one who spreads strife among brothers"* Proverbs 6:16-17 & 19.
- **The spirit of an unbeliever.** *"But if any one does not provide for his own, and especially for those of his household, he has denied the faith, and is worse than an unbeliever"* 1 Timothy 5:8.
- **Lacking the love of Christ.** *"So husbands ought to love their own wives as their own bodies. He who loves his own wife loves himself"* Ephesians 5:28.

Verbal outbursts have consequences and are a manifestation of deeper issues within the person who lacks self-control with this emotion. Ultimately, they are in a state of idolatry and the root cause is unbelief in God's love for them.

People who make verbal outbursts are easy to spot. They are the ones who get red in the face, raise their voices to a booming pitch, and say all kinds of nasty, insulting things when they are angry. People who use this technique are highly frustrated. They have strong feelings, yet they fell as though they are not taken seriously. Most of these people have tried to express their anger calmly, but for some reason or another, it didn't work. As a last resort they verbally blast their victims to inflict some pain. Their unconscious goal is to make the other person fell so badly that he cannot help but respond in the 'correct' way.

Some of these people have legitimate complaints that cause them to feel like blasting away. Most will say that they feel misunderstood. They will say that the reason they resort to such outbursts is to get the undivided attention of the person who has made them feel rejected. At the same time, however, many of these people are slow to admit that when they express anger, they have one and only one response they wish to hear. The reason that they make violent outbursts is that they did not get their specified response. They are asking for total submission rather than honest communication.

The ultimate form of blasting is physical violence. Acts of physical violence virtually always begin with verbal cheap shots. Once people allow their anger to grow to this point, it is hard to control the urge to physically "put someone in his place." This only accomplishes the opposite of healthy relationships. It builds thick, high walls.

Obstacles to Repentance

One of the great inhibitors of true repentance is stubborn self-sufficiency. We want to be masters of our own lives while saying all the while that Jesus is Lord yet never coming to a true understanding of His Lordship. Projectionism makes a declaration of independence from God, leaning on our own strategies for meeting our desperate need for affirmation and safety.

Even though the Father calls us to walk at times in dark places, trusting in His Word, and relying on His leading through the Holy Spirit, we have lit our own torches so that we can see for ourselves the path ahead. This causes God's discipline on us as described in Isaiah 50:10-11, *"You will lie down in torment."*

Refusing to examine our innate self-centeredness, we remain committed to changing our circumstances, intent on winning others approval or respect yet we fail miserably only to repeat the cycle again. We fail to distinguish between the legitimate desire for change and the illegitimate demand of

God and others to become what we need. We have entered a life of idolatry.

The three most common mistakes in these circumstances in shedding light on change are (1) our self-diagnosis is that we have only a minor problem; (2) our self-prognosis is that it is curable by our efforts; and (3) our self-treatment is to redouble our efforts to get others to change so that we won't be in so much pain. Jeremiah 17:9 reminds us that our hearts are *"deceitful above all things, and desperately wicked."* We cannot love at all, and even with His Spirit indwelling us, we struggle with a nature that insistently drives us to self-protection. We must be willing to admit this deep-rooted propensity to utterly selfish living if we are to know joyous release of true repentance and forgiveness.

Deception needs Revelation

Deception at its core definition is idolatry. Deceptive people are into manipulating, controlling, and self-worshipping. For this reason, God has given them over to their sinful ways and allowed depravity to enter into their minds (Romans 1:21-26). *"And we know that the judgment of God rightly falls upon those who practice such things"* Romans 2:2.

The deception of uncontrolled anger lies in the user's justification in manifesting it. They are engaged in an activity they describe as being loving yet their love is based on conditions and not unconditional grace and mercy. If a person does not conform to their demands, then they have no need for a communicative relationship with them. This thrusts them into an immature behavior called the 'Silent Treatment.' All chance of communication is shut down until further notice. In most cases, they will never broach the subject again and likely return as if nothing ever happened in the first place. The tornado came through ripped the town apart and then sunny skies have returned leaving an emotional mess behind.

The wrong dynamics are being used by the person bringing the outburst of anger; no doubt. However, unless the person with the uncontrolled anger gets to a place where they are forced to see the error of their ways or comes to hate their behavior it could take years before any resolution is maintained. Broken relationships, divorce, lost jobs and ministries, even at times, arrest and conviction leading to jail can be the dirty resume of the angry person. These are life altering choices. Yet, God has not given up. He who began a good work in them will see it to completion (Phil. 1:6).

God makes Himself known to us by revelation (Eph. 3:13). In that, forgetting what lies behind we may push on to the upward call of God in Christ Jesus (Phil. 3:13-14). Since the Lord is not finished constructing us into the image of His Son, Jesus Christ, we can be assured that He will continue to work in the heart by revelation of the person with uncontrolled anger. Revelation casts out deception. Revelation opens the eyes of the believer who is deceived shedding light onto a dark situation. Pray for revelation that leads to true repentance.

Our re-parenting with a New Purpose

True repentance requires two things: (1) recognizing the sinful purpose of our lives to stay out of pain by protecting ourselves in any way we can and (2) embracing a new purpose to utterly trust God for our inner lives by dropping our self-protection and moving with openness toward life according to God's legitimacy in it. This we must do without making excuses or projecting our failure to love on others and

God. Before God, there is no excuse for breaking His commandments.

Walking a life with Jesus as our Lord gives purpose to our existence and meaning to our life's work. A born-again life establishes a re-parenting of our lives from our natural birth parents to our supernatural birth Father God. He is constantly at work through the Holy Spirit to conform our lives from the low self-esteem of the past into a Christ-like nature going forward. He is working out our salvation and giving us hope to end the treadmill of hurt and pain in our lives.

The natural man's reaction to being shown his faults is resentment, denial, or self-defense, but those who lives are exercised by godly repentance actively seek to know how they are not being loving in a certain circumstance, so they can repent, receive God's grace through Christ, and choose to change.

This kind of repentance is possible only to those who know what it means to live by grace, forgiven of sins of unlove by the boundless mercy of God because of Jesus' death on the cross. If we will receive the love and forgiveness of God, His re-parenting nature toward us, then we must also repent of our self-protection and move into genuine openness in our relationships with others as well.

Summing Up

In dealing with our low self-esteem and self-protectionist nature repentance is an essential internal exercise, a change of mind or purpose that happens in our hearts. God also calls us to live out our repentance behaviorally, excising from our lives by the power of the Holy Spirit the old self-protective habits of living for other's approval or of controlling others so they will meet our needs. When we repent of our sinful self-protection and lack of love, certain behaviors will appear in our lives that will reveal to us and others the genuine repentance of our hearts.

This will be the internal battle of your mind and of your life. It requires the desire for change. It requires an attitude that is Christ-like in every way. It does not happen overnight but is a habitual exercise in the power of God's love. It is approaching life from a vertical upward surge to the throne of grace no matter what our natural eyesight, set on the horizontal aspects of life, sees in our path of daily existence. Trust in Him, trust in His grace and mercy. Trust in His desire to change you into the indwelling power of the life of His Son, our Lord Jesus Christ through the Holy Spirit.

4

Driving in Circles

"The way of a fool is right in his own eyes, but a wise man is he who listens to counsel" Prov. 12:15.

One of the enemy's greatest weapons against us is to lead us around the mountain of life as many times as he possibly can. His strategy is to never let us learn the process of God's redemption. In doing so the person with uncontrolled anger cannot attain a spiritual walk that enters into the fullest potential of God's plan for their life. They are *"always learning and never able to come to the knowledge of the truth"* 2 Tim. 3:7.

There are habitual elements in the life of people with uncontrolled anger that causes them to repeat their sinfulness time and again. An angry person does not necessarily start the day in their mind to be angry. It's quite the opposite. They are thrust into a situation that by some unbeknownst circumstance to them they had no foreknowledge would occur or by something that recently occurred. It may have been something that was discovered about them that they were called into account for without prior knowledge and asked to reconcile it or to give explanation. When this happens a defense-mechanism is instinctively placed into action. The more they are pressured to give explanation the more heated the discussion that will ensue. If the explanations are not accepted and they are pressed further the anger wells up in them and as a last resort they will explode with an uncontrolled emotion of anger. This is from the frustration they are feeling that they are not believed or loved or respected. Their actions in these situations instinctively turn to anger rather than the biblical instructions given to us by the Lord.

Trapped

The foundation laid for the person of uncontrolled anger is set firmly in dysfunction and because they do not have a roadmap or plan to rid themselves of the dysfunction in which many cases they are too deceived to see it clearly for themselves they are trapped in a vicious circle of repeated spats of anger. These occurrences are habitual and unless broken they will destroy everything in the path of the person carrying themselves in this disposition. *"The snare of the bird catcher is in all their ways, and there is only hostility in the house of God. They have gone deep in depravity...He will remember their iniquity, He will punish their sins"* Hosea 9:8-9.

In Hosea 9:9 the word tells us God will remember iniquity and punish sin because of the depth of the depravity. For the born-again believer, we know our sins are forgiven. How then is this word fulfilled in the life of an angry believer? In 2018, I counseled a ministry leader who was having issues in his THIRD marriage. He had uncontrollable anger and used every justification for it—*she made me do it, I don't like people getting in my face, she doesn't submit*—you name it he had the reason to justify his anger. Never once was repentance a part of his vocabulary. After his explosions he would ask forgiveness only to walk in the same bad behavior of anger.

Never changing, never allowing the Spirit of God to make him more like Jesus in his marriage, his family relationships, or in his character. He stood on his diluted understanding of the Scriptures to justify his position. He was deceived. His depravity clouded his judgment. His high-mindedness would not allow him to see the error of his ways. His wife has since left him and he has moved on to seek another relationship with the possibility of a FOURTH wife. In refusing to take heed to wise counsel I dare say he will walk this road the remainder of his life until the Lord brings him to a place of repentance for his outbursts of anger.

"…for the anger of man does not achieve the righteousness of God"
James 1:20.

The sinfulness Hosea is speaking of with the believer has everything to do with repeated bad choices, never entering the place of God's choosing, and hitting a spiritual ceiling that keeps them from moving into a greater realm of God's kingdom. This is the punishment Hosea is speaking to; a never ending cycle of repeated habitual sin that keeps us from growing in Christ.

High mindedness

"Knowledge makes arrogant, but love edifies" 1 Cor. 8:1. The presence of high mindedness in a person is a sure sign that they are walking in circles in their life's journey. It is a masking of low self-esteem. They have love issues. They have developed a steel wall around themselves to protect the hurt in them concerning love issues. At the core of this belief system is their unbelief in God's love for them. They do not believe in His unconditional love toward them. It is likely they

grew up in a household where love was conditional. Since we get our understanding of God's love for us through our relationship with our fathers, it is safe to conclude that the high minded person never received unconditional love from their father.

Low Self-esteem

Satan's deadliest weapon against the church is low self-esteem. Our self-esteem is either the crippler or the completer of our relationships, ministries, and walk with the Lord. If our emotions are damaged to the point of despair then we have been driving in circles most of our Christian life. Only through understanding God's love *(agapeo)* can we expect to walk a full and fruitful life.

When low self-esteem is present in us it effects every aspect of who we are and what we can become. A person with low self-esteem desires intimacy but never attains the full satisfaction thereof. Instead they will develop habits of intimate release through other means; pornography, adultery, masturbation, fantasy, and every other form of the flesh. They desire to be close to the people they are in relationship with however because of the deception of their self-esteem issues they can never attain satisfaction. They need a revelation of God's love obtained through the power of the Holy Spirit and supported by the infallibility of His Word.

Debt Collecting

Unforgiveness is the underlying motivation in the attitude of the debt collector. A wrong done against them is held in a secret place of a debt owed only to be taken out and placed on the altar of unforgiveness at a time of uncontrollable anger to be collected so that they can win the argument and think they have taken the field of battle. The debt or wrong done against them could have happened years ago. It doesn't matter when it was stored in their memory of indebted accounts it is raised time and again without even an inkling of forgiveness. This is their weapon of choice. It is used to control and manipulate those they are angry with so that they might get their own way in the matter. It is fellowshipping with a spirit of witchcraft!

When the debt collector holds a wrong done against them they are as the slave who was forgiven his debt by the king yet refused to forgive the one who owed him as told in Matthew 18:21-35. *"But the slave went out and found one of his fellow-slaves who owed him a hundred denarii; and he seized him and began to choke him, saying, 'Pay back what you owe.' So his fellow-slave fell down and began to entreat him, saying, 'Have patience with me and I will repay you.' He was unwilling however, but went and threw him in prison until he should pay back what was owed"* Matt. 18:28-30. When it was told to the king what the slave had done the king summoned the slave immediately before his presence and demanded an answer.

God is extremely serious about the act of forgiveness. He does not tolerate an unforgiving spirit because the cross of Christ has paid the debt for everyone's sin. We should be a no-judgment zone of God's witness in our walks, ministries, and relationships no matter what has occurred. We have no right to hold a debt no matter how justified we believe the circumstances to be. This is a hard word! But it is a true word. It is a truth that sets our souls and spirits free from the bondages that would bind us. **If we do not forgive we will not be forgiven** (see Matt. 18:32-35). *"So shall the heavenly Father also do to you, if each of you does not forgive his brother from your heart"* Matt. 34-35.

The Lord's instruction concerning *debt-collecting* does not end with the teaching of Matthew 18:21-35. Jesus teaches us how to pray and gives us the Lord's prayer in Matt. 6:8-13. In v12 a condition is presented to us and specifically to the debt collector. *"And forgive us our debts, as we also have forgiven our debtors"* Matt. 6:12. Jesus is very specific in His teaching adding an emphasis on forgiveness and the Father's attitude toward that action in v14-15, *"For if you forgive men for their transgressions, your heavenly Father will also forgive you. But if you do not forgive men, then your Father will not forgive your transgressions."*

We know that the blood of Jesus Christ has given us restoration to the Father and our accepting and confessing Him as Lord secures our salvation through the Holy Spirit. Therefore, what can Jesus have meant by saying if you do not forgive then your sins are also not forgiven? I am not so convinced that He is speaking to a salvation issue on this subject. Although, He had not yet gone to the cross when He spoke these words. So for the unbeliever it is a salvation issue. However, to those of us who already walk in the saving grace of Christ the meaning of Matthew 6 and 18 has to have a different interpretation. The forgiving of our transgressions are eternally washed white as snow concerning our eternity yet in this life many of us still walk in bondage to our sin because of unforgiveness in our hearts. This bondage keeps us in a place where God cannot promote us, bless us, or otherwise anoint us for the work of His Kingdom to the levels of the Holy Spirit's intentions or desires. Harboring unforgiveness keeps us in a pit that God had no intention of seeing us there. It clouds our judgments, hinders our ministry, and destroys our relationships. Most medical professionals now tell us that unforgiveness is the cause of many physical disorders such as stress, anxiety, arthritis, and heart failure.

Debt collecting is a stronghold that even though we believe by deceptive practices that we have justice on our side causes us to walk around the mountain driving in circles again and again.

Difficulties in Intimacy

This is a condition of the flesh that can never be resolved without the revelation of God's *(agapeo)* love for us. It is a wheel within a wheel. We drive in circles by repeated motives of the flesh and still we continue the same practice never changing our behavior for lack of revelation knowledge. There are four crippling aspects of intimacy difficulties.

- **Fear of vulnerability**. The people who walk in this dysfunction are afraid of getting hurt and showing any vulnerability to expose their heart. They've trusted before only to have been disappointed. They started out in their relationship vulnerable and willing to be open only to have been rejected for it. The cause of this reaction to their rejection is because they placed their hopes and eyes on the wrong prize. Men will disappoint you, Jesus never will. We must open our hearts to God in order to experience the fullest relationship possible to Him. Even when men hurt us and relationships fail us, the Lord is faithful to carry us through. He never disappoints!
- **Fear of judgment**. Low self-esteem dictates this fear. We will act and behave in a certain manner just to avoid being judged by someone. Our life is operating on a stage with the curtain drawn. We never want anyone to see what is behind the curtain on our stage of life. Our thinking is if they see us as we truly are then we will be judged and never attain the blessings of our

relationship. The fallacy in this thinking is that the Lord already knows every aspect of our lives and He has ordered our steps. Our unbelief in His eternal love for us is what keeps us driving in circles.

- **The path of secrecy.** Since nothing behind the curtain of our life can be revealed because of lack of trust and unbelief it is essential to keep our sins hidden and in a secret place. Even our relationships and the faults we display in those relationships are to be kept under wraps. The person of low self-esteem lives a life of secrecy. They cannot have any of the desires of their flesh exposed. The misnomer in this fact is that the character they display will certainly expose their sin no matter how secret they try to keep it. Wondering eyes, immaturity in personality, arrogance, pornography, adultery, all manners of the flesh, and a lack of empathy toward others are all examples of the bad character portrayed in high mindedness. Those who walk in this manner are desperate for love, approval, and a release of the stress, anxiety, and pressures of a life lived in secrecy. They are not aware of God's true love and acceptance for them. In their minds they speak of God's love for them but in their hearts they have yet to come to the realization of it.

- **Fear of rejection.** This is an unbelief in God's love. The life of a person of uncontrolled anger places rejection at the core of its main foundation. In doing so they labor upon it for years building an altar and a temple in their hearts of rejection. They are desperate to be loved and not believing they are they seek it in many other places just to receive the falsehood of a lust disguising itself as love even if only for a moment.

Once it has reached its fulfillment they are immediately on another quest repeating the same process. They are driving in circles.

Revelation is the only spiritual weapon that can break the bondage of uncontrolled anger, low self-esteem, and high mindedness. There needs to be a desire for change. When that happens the Holy Spirit is faithful in creating an atmosphere for change and bringing to us the realization of the love of the Father. In some instances it can only happen through deliverance. Spiritual forces have entered the lives of some where deliverance is required. A door to the world of evil was opened at some point in their lives and it needs to be closed. This can only happen through prayer, repentance, and the covered blood of Jesus Christ sealed in the Holy Spirit of promise. Standing on God's Word is key to the healing process.

5

Failed Relationships

"...If a man be caught in any trespass, you who are spiritual, restore such a one in a spirit of gentleness..."
Gal. 6:1

In an earlier chapter I discussed a minister who came to me for counsel and was disposing of his third wife. He had already begun to move onto a fourth woman. He refused to heed counsel and instead justified his actions by misinterpreting God's word. He spoke of all the men of God who had more than one wife and still had anointed ministries. He used Samson as his justification for his immorality and wondering eyes. He claimed his anger to be righteous indignation and not sin. His call to me was to get agreement in divorcing his third wife and when I would only speak of reconciliation I knew he had already made his decision. He just wanted agreement by unveiling his checklist of her deficiencies which he believed justified his separation. In speaking with his wife her attitude was to reconcile but she was not going to live with an abusive angry man the rest of her life. She wanted him to seek counsel and that was the reason for his call. Also, they called me because I do not run in his circle of ministry friends where he would be mortified if they knew of his anger issues.

In so many cases, the problem can be fixed and reconciliation obtained when the Lord is involved in the decision process. This particular minister is an Apostle over 46 different churches, he ministers on 5 different Christian television broadcasts, on three different Continents, over 50 different mega-churches, and is a constant guest minister for some very large international ministries raising $millions in the process. It is this resume that is the issue in him not being able to receive the correct counsel needed. He is incorrectly judging the size of his ministry as approval from God rather than correctly discerning that our life is to be transformed into the image of Christ. It's all about character building! In this, he is left wanting.

We mistakenly as a church believe that magnetic personalities translate to be anointing. On one of my ministry tours I discerned a spirit of homosexuality in three men who were preaching, singing, and prophesying in the services. When addressing the issue with the leadership their response was, "they are anointed." I told them not to mistake anointing for talent. Eloquent speech, good teaching, and those who can ignite an audience does not mean they are anointed especially when they are walking in unrepented sin. Unrepented sin brings about death and it will quickly unleash itself in a relationship.

Law bound legalism

"Where there is a lot of law there is little love."
Edwin Cole, Maximized Manhood.

Uncontrolled anger personalities administer the law in their relationships more than any other. It is their way of controlling those around them and creating a false sense of security. In many respects they are literalists when conversing and communicating with others. I recently counseled a man who would explain his situation trying to justify his anger toward his spouse. As I reiterated his conversation with me and asked probing questions concerning the events surrounding his uncontrolled anger he would deny certain descriptions of the event until I discerned he was a literalist justifying his actions. The conversation played out in this way; Q. *"Why did you lose your temper at your brothers-in-law's wedding causing your wife to have a difficult time?* A. *I didn't lose my temper **at the wedding**.* His wife disagreed, and we finally realized it wasn't at the event itself but in the hotel room for 6 hours of ranting and raving, threatening divorce, and tossing his wedding ring at her. Q. *"What made you lose your temper **in the hotel room** at your brothers-in-law's wedding?* A. *"She made me angry."* I received a straight answer when I posed the question in an exact manner relating the event. Although we were discussing events concerning things that took place at the wedding unless I posed literal questions of exact events I wasn't going to get a straight answer.

In his mind he had done nothing wrong in how he answered the question posed to him. There was no guile in his answer. His high mindedness set the tone and the reasoning for him in the counseling session. His low self-esteem is on an automatic defense mechanism. When certain catch phrases or tones in conversation toward him are discerned in his mind, he immediately puts up a steel wall to feel a false sense of security, protection. He feels the need to defend and justify himself. He is operating from a place of deception that has been the norm for him for many years because of past circumstances leading him to believe it is normal behavior. This mindset has to be broken in him and the foundation he has laid for his marital relationship torn down and reset with the Word of God. He needs a revelation of who the Holy Spirit really is in his life. He needs to be led to the altar of God's eternal love; the cross of Jesus Christ. It will take work. It is not an immediate fix. However, if he is not willing to realize he needs change he will continue to have failed relationships.

Mood swings

Another man I counseled was divorcing his third wife. His anger had gotten the best of their relationship only after two years of marriage. His way of controlling the relationships in his life was through an angry spirit. Everyone in his household walked on eggshells daily when he was around. He was explosive. However, at times, he could be gentle and loving. His wife and children never knew when the volcano in him was going to erupt. It could happen over the slightest thing. Just asking how his day was or where he had spent the day would set him off depending on what was going on his mind at any particular moment. He had mood swings stemming from his low self-esteem. He did not love himself how then could he love anyone else. *"So husbands ought to love their own wives as their own bodies. He who loves his own wife loves himself"* Eph. 5:28. This type of uncontrolled anger in someone needs deliverance and they have to learn to forgive themselves to be set free.

Spiritual Battles

"For that which I am doing, I do not understand; for I am not practicing what I would like to do, but I am doing the very thing I hate" Romans 7:15.

The struggle in the life of people of uncontrolled anger is so enormous that they are coming against spiritual giants that have ruled over them for years. They need to be set free.

The Spirit sets itself against the flesh and only walking in the understanding of the Spirit of God can we obtain victory from the things of the flesh. *"For the law of the Spirit of life (the Holy Spirit) in Christ Jesus has set you free from the law of sin and of death"* Romans 8:2. It is only through the Holy Spirit dwelling in us can we overcome the sinfulness of the flesh. We need to give control of our minds [souls] (the battlefield between spirit and flesh) to the Holy Spirit. There is no other way to liberty.

"For the mind set on the flesh is death, but the mind set on the Spirit is life and peace" Romans 8:6.

When our minds are set on the things of the flesh we are hostile toward God. However, since our conversion to a born-again life we no longer walk in the flesh but rather in the Spirit (Romans 8:7).

Effects of the Law of the flesh and the Law of the Spirit

We live in both realms of flesh and Spirit. Each one battles the other over our lifetime. Our decision-making process in each of these realms determines the effectiveness in our lives either negative or positive. How does the choice we make affect us in this life?

- **Our jobs. Negatively;** based on the choice we make to live a failed life directly affects the type of employment we seek. Those who cannot sustain successful relationships will seek opportunities to satisfy their hunger to be accepted, acknowledged, and given credit in their life in areas that best pay homage to their dysfunction. In doing so, they ignore the call of God on their lives to serve the kingdom of God in the capacity the Lord has desired for them. I have seen men called to ministry fulltime but because of low self-esteem they sought employment elsewhere to trump up a euphoric feeling and offset the dysfunction they were experiencing. They still served in ministry but only in a limited capacity because they allowed the distraction of their other employment to take top priority. When Jesus called the disciples to ministry they left their nets behind.

Positively; Other people, once called to serve Him, left everything behind concerning matters of the world and pursued fulltime ministry work. In doing so, they have reaped the blessing of the Lord because they submitted to the Law of the Spirit and denied the Law of the flesh.

- **Our Relationships. Negatively;** the Law of the flesh brings a struggle that looks to tear down all that God has intended for good. When a person's low self-esteem feeds into this law it is fuel for evil, discord, and an anti-Christ spirit. Its spiritual core is witchcraft. The love God would have us display in our relationships become tainted and discolored. Our thoughts wander into a fantasy world that seemly fools us into thinking we have relief yet it is only a pit of despair. Our desire for intimacy is never realized. The flesh brings no good deed only destruction and false hope. Our prayers go unanswered. Our gifts are stagnant and our ministry stalls. Depression sets in.

  Positively; the Law of the Spirit brings peace, joy, freedom, and liberty. God's prosperity is abundant, and His blessings do not cease. Our relationships are strong having our eyes set upon the Lord. Our prayer life is abundant, praise and worship are upon our lips, and the Word of God is strongly set within our hearts. Unity is our covering in Christ. In that unity comes anointing and His glory upon us. When this is present in our relationships the supernatural power of God is upon us. God's train fills our temple and His throne sits, reigns, and rules in our hearts.

- **Our ministry. Negatively;** the Law of the flesh causes us to see only in the natural when it pertains to spiritual matters. We serve God with rose colored glasses never getting the clear picture of His kingdom blessing. The work for Christ is merely a religious gesture, ritualistic and pharisaical. We approach life from a hard place that gives no way to empathy or grace. Our sight only displays black and white areas. We have no room in our lives to see the gray. There is only judgment through right and wrong. Our justification is based on a hard interpretation of the Word. We have no time for mercy. Inside the person with low self-esteem is the desperate cry for mercy, grace, relief from the agony of a life of continued hardness of the Law. They do not know how to achieve it having no knowledge or understanding of the love of God.

  Positively; the law of the Spirit brings power and anointing into the ministry. Souls are saved. The gospel is preached with the power of the Holy Spirit and the gifts flow in the ministry. The character of Jesus Christ is ever-present through the Law of the Spirit. We fulfill Galatians 5:22-23, *"But the fruit of the Spirit is love, joy, peace, patience, kindness, goodness, faithfulness, gentleness, self-control; against such things there is no law."*

Failed Relationships are the result of uncontrolled anger, high-mindedness, low self-esteem, depression, and immorality

(Gal. 5:19-21). Those who choose to remain walking in these things are fellowshipping with a witchcraft spirit. An idolatrous nature is what leads them to this end. There choice is to worship themselves rather than the Creator who is blessed forever (Romans 1).

Deception and depravity are no excuse as to why someone walks in high-mindedness, low self-esteem, and uncontrolled anger. *"Do not be deceived, God is not mocked; for whatever a man sows, this he will also reap. For the one who sows to his own flesh shall from the flesh reap corruption, but the one who sows to the Spirit shall from the Spirit reap eternal life"* Gal. 6:7-8.

Building Self-Esteem in Failed Relationships

There are several spiritual principles in building self-esteem to those who in failed relationships. I concur that these principles could even be used in relationships that are not in failure and I encourage you to practice them.

- **Offer Total Acceptance.** There is power in unconditional love. It is liberty to the one receiver and the giver. It is God's heart. Power statements are a useful tool to help in establishing non-judgmental acceptance in the life of the person suffering from failed relationships. For instance, *"I love you for who you are not for what you do"* and *"I am so glad you are a part of us."* Inclusion is always a powerful tool of acceptance in a person's life.
- **Keep Life Manageable.** Encourage them to set realistic goals. Offer prayer support and spiritual exhortation.
- **Deal with Difficult Times.** Let God give you the strength to be supportive of them in difficult times especially during their lapse of judgment.
- **Build a Sense of Destiny.** Pray for God's defining

purpose in their lives. Encourage them in their gifting.
- **Provide the Freedom to Fail.** Give them an assurance of acceptance regardless of their performance. Show God's unconditional love and support. *"...speak to men for edification and exhortation and consolation"* 1 Cor. 14:3.

Words have power

The life of a person with uncontrolled anger have received words that have placed a curse or death upon them. Words have the power to contaminate a positive self-image or to heal the spreading malignancy of a negative one. Words become powerful seeds. Once planted, they take root and bear fruit in season. If negative, the result is a life of anger and resentment. If positive, a healthy self-image and a life that will bless others and not curse.

"Death and life are in the power of the tongue" Proverbs 18:21.

In fact, many of the mistaken perceptions about themselves have sprouted from others' negative words. These bad seeds have been around since the fall of Adam and Eve in the Garden. In life, from time to time, they have crossed over into the field of those displaying anger in the form of bad jokes, criticisms, and rejection. Others have occurred from bad parenting, worldly values, and cultural decay.

Planting Good Seeds

We share in God's handiwork when we use words that give life to a person's self-esteem. In Christian relationships one of the most important things is what we say and share with one another. When positive words flow, the relationships are robust and flourishing. If the lines of communication go down permanently, it is only a matter of time before that relationship dies. We can create life in our brothers and sisters with positive words, or we can inflict destruction with our negative or neglectful ones.

Sow Words of Praise

The definition of praise is to give value, to extol, to magnify, to honor, to commend, and to applaud. If you would give some creative thought to the words in that definition, you could come up with a hundred different ways to praise the person suffering from low self-esteem. Praise is a necessary tool in the process of helping a person of low self-esteem to heal. The more we give verbal expression of gratitude or praise to that person the more secure they will become in their self-esteem. It places them on a road of healing in letting go of their anger.

Attitudes of Apathy and Complacency

Apathy. It is rare for someone to be apathetic (defined as someone who shows no interest or emotion) when doing something for a person when they have a genuine desire to be kind and helpful. It does not necessarily mean an apathetic individual is being aggressive. Naturally, some apathy is normal. Some psychologists insist however, that there is no such thing as innocent apathy. A person who has a well-ingrained pattern of apathy probably can be categorized as someone with an anger problem.

Apathy can be a convenient way to punish someone for not being the kind of person that they "ought" to be in the mind of the person with apathy. One man I counseled was constantly showing apathy in doing little favors that his wife would ask him to do. When he finally got up the courage to speak his mind, this man said that it didn't bother him that he was apathetic. He resented the way his wife nagged him, so he didn't want to do anything kind for her anyway. Rather than dealing with his resentment, he repressed it and let his anger turn to apathy.

Notice what apathy can communicate. Like other forms of passive-aggressive behavior, it can be a way of stating that other people's desires are not very high on the priority list. Chronic apathy is a sure-fire indicator of the 'don't-care' attitude. Apathetic people often offer weak excuses about events or responsibilities in their mind. However, if they were asked to do something for a person of imminent importance there would be little doubt whether it would get done. Apathy is a way of asserting that one does not share the same priorities with other people.

Complacency. This behavior is marked by self-satisfaction especially when accompanied by unawareness of actual deficiencies. We all have been in situations that we wished we could escape from. In fact, if we don't watch ourselves we can easily become angry for having to put us with circumstances that are not to our liking. A classic example of this kind of anger is the intelligent child who makes poor grades in school not because of his inability but because of boredom. This type of person underscores their anger by believing themselves to be content where they are as the whole world around them is moving on.

This passive-aggressive behavior is an indication that a person is disgusted with the circumstances around them. Rather than being honest with anger, the complacent person prefers to be insulting by drifting off into a world all their own. They are communicating that what to have nothing to do with anyone else. Their life is more important that the needs of those around them. This is a stubborn way of demanding that people leave them alone.

Every one of these aspects of a person with uncontrolled anger can be present at any one time in their personality. It certainly is a cause to their failed relationships. Identifying these character flaws is the beginning of the healing process. Each one of these characteristics must be covered in the blood of Jesus Christ, prayed through in the power of the Holy Spirit, and brought to confession for deliverance.

"...for with the heart man believes, resulting in righteousness, and with the mouth he confesses, resulting in salvation" Romans 10:10.

6

A Cracked Foundation

"Behold, I lay in Zion a choice stone, a precious corner stone, and he who believes in Him shall not be disappointed" 1 Peter 2:6.

In Matthew 7:24-27 the Lord gives us a description of two foundations; one built on the rock and the other on sand. He says in v24, *"…everyone who hears these words…and acts upon them, may be compared to a wise man, who built his house upon the rock."* There are three key biblical principles in this verse that must be practiced daily to obtain a victorious life **on the rock.**

1. **Hear** these words. *"So faith comes from hearing, and hearing by the word of Christ"* Romans 10:17. Standing on the promise of God's word to complete the good work He began in us and to bring it to perfection (Phil. 1:6) is an essential belief in realizing God's healing in our lives.

2. **Act** upon them (the words). *"Prove yourselves doers of the word, and not merely hearers who delude themselves"* James 1:22. It is not enough for us to just hear the Good News of Jesus Christ without putting action to the hearing and accepting Him as Lord. A firm spiritual foundation is dependent upon such things.

3. **Build the house on the rock.** *"...Thou art the Christ, the Son of the Living God...and upon this rock I will build My church: and the gates of Hades shall not overpower it"* Matt. 16:16 & 18. All solid foundations must be set upon a solid cornerstone otherwise through years of decay, the storms of life, and the shifting of earthly things corrosion and mayhem will most assuredly occur.

At the cross the Lord defeated every spiritual and temporal dysfunction of body, soul, and spirit. Even the fall of creation was covered in His shed blood and work at the cross. Jesus gave us every hope to walk a healthy and emotionally healed life. Our surrendering to Him sets in motion the inner workings of the Holy Spirit. We have taken within ourselves the life of our Eternal Father. Our inheritance is set, and our adoption secured.

"See how great a love the Father has bestowed upon us, that we should be called children of God and such we are" 1 John 3:1.

In being like Him (1 John 3:2) our faith rests in the knowledge that *"[our] hope fixed on Him purifies himself, just as He is pure"* 1 John 3:3.

He has placed a secure and solid foundation of hope in our lives. If we stand on this promise and become more like Him through the working power of the presence of the Holy Spirit in us, we will have the emotional healing that has kept us in bondage to low self-esteem.

On the Sand

Again, in Matthew 7:26-27, *"And everyone who hears*

these words of mine and does not act upon them, will be like a foolish man, who built his house upon the sand. And the rain descended, and the floods came, and the winds blew, and burst against that house; and it fell, and great was its fall." The biblical principles are the same as those demonstrated in Matthew 7:25; **hear, act, and build.** However, the practice of hear, act, and build are set on temporal activities and responses.

We hear, act, and build by horizontal sight and respond to that situation based on our carnal knowledge causing wrong motivations to determine unsolvable outcomes. These outcomes cause us to walk in circles never learning the process. They set in motion the dysfunctional responses of our cracked foundation based on our past. These dynamics bring the uncontrolled anger in our personality to the surface. This is the house built on the sand. Great is its fall!

A wise man builds on the rock of salvation; Jesus Christ. A foolish man builds on the sand and loses his salvation. One endures against the enemy's attacks and victory is in his camp, the other succumbs to the attacks and lives a defeated life.

The Attacks of the Enemy

The rain, the floods, and the wind all beat against the house mentioned in this teaching. There is no difference whether it beats against the house on a rock or the house built on sand except one stand against the attack. Each attack comes in its season. If you are aware of weather patterns certain natural elements appear at predicted times of the year based on the season. The enemy's attacks against us are no different. They are strategic spiritually and manifest in the natural. Always in season. Asia has its rainy season. Europe its winter weather patterns. Africa its droughts. These elements are patterns that appear and can be predicted based on past occurrences. The attacks on our lives are similar in the understanding of these weather patterns. If you are walking in a season of blessing, the attacks will come. If you are in a season of spiritual drought, the attacks will come. If you are in a season of physical distress, the attacks will come. No matter what season of your life the enemy is always at war with you. The difference of success and victory is dependent upon where your house is built; on the rock or on sand.

There is no stopping the coming attacks no more than we can stop the weather from occurring. We are in a spiritual war over our very souls. But rejoice, the victory is ours through Jesus Christ! We can endure the coming onslaught and walk away unscathed. The secret to our emotional healing lies in becoming more like Jesus Christ. Applying God's Word to our situation and standing on His promises brings about the victory.

Characteristics of a Cracked Foundation

The Silent Treatment. There is no rule that states a person must be boisterous when angry. Anger can take various forms of expression in subtle ways. Silent anger can be very effective if one's goal is to "even the score" with someone else. When you examine the silent treatment closely, you will find that it is the most controlling form of anger that there is.

This method of anger is a total and complete breakdown in the lines of communication. Keep in mind that even though the lines of communication are not expressed verbally it doesn't mean that they are not communicating! If you observe their behavior, they are speaking loud and clear just not with verbal expression! Most of those who put this method to practice feel a sense of betrayal and therefore justify the use of the silent treatment. After there anger has subsided they return to the scene believing no justification or asking of forgiveness is necessary in resuming their relationship to the one they were punishing. Someone who remains stubbornly silent when it is clear that a verbal exchange is needed is communicating a great deal of anger.

"Silence is a way of stating that the other person is not worthy enough to talk to." Dr. Les Carter, "Getting the Best of Your Anger"

The person using the silent treatment method usually excuses this behavior by saying they wish to have no part of a circular argument. But they are actually creating a feud that resembles the legendary Hatfield and McCoys. They forgot why they were angry with each other but know they believe they have good reason. In addition, the feud may have been over some silly reason as simple as stealing a pig.

This behavior causes harm to the one practicing it. There is no constructive resolution to the action of this behavior and in the end, all involved are fighting a losing proposition.

Procrastination. There is a sinking feeling in the person who is a procrastinator. They are in a state of not being able to control their environment and have no solution to their problem. They are in stuck in the "I" mentality. Self-absorption is a passive-aggression behavior. Rather than seeking help or asking for assistance they let the problem at hand sit hoping time will solve their dilemma; out of sight, out of mind mentality wins the day.

In Mark 4:35-41, Jesus was ministering to the crowds at the sea of Galilee. When it was completed He said to the disciples, *"let us go over to the other side"* v.35. In the middle of the sea a great storm arose, and the waves began to fill the boat. The disciples became afraid thinking Jesus had brought them out to the sea to die. Jesus was asleep in the boat. When they awoke Him, He commanded the storm to be silent. Immediately the wind died down and seas became calm. They arrived on the other side of the sea unscathed.

The biblical principle when troubles occurs is not to ignore it, not to skirt around it, but to embrace it head on and let God bring you through it! Face the dilemma knowing that the Lord is with you and He will protect you. He is your strong tower (Ps. 61:3). Jesus brought the disciples through the storm not around it!

Depression. Many people are surprised to learn that depression is simply a form of anger. It settles in our spirit after years of disappointment and rejection. Moving from one failure in life to another repeatedly causes repressed anger to settle in us and bury our hurtful emotion deep within. The depressed person passively communicates that they have found no good in the world and in an act of aggression they withdraw from others. It is a form of selfishness because they are not allowing others to learn what is needed to help the relationship. In all fairness, some depression can be chemical. In most cases, it is usually a passive way for a person to check-out from dealing with their feelings day-to-day.

Depressed people believe they are in a world without hope. Their future is believed to be a certain doom. It is a dark and unsettled place. Their minds are filled with thoughts of suicide and hopelessness. They are in utter despair. The only way back to end this depressive spirit is the Word of God applied to their situation. Make no mistake, it is a spiritual battle however, the Word of God gives victory.

In 1 Kings 19:4, Elijah contemplates death for himself. He is praying to the Lord and trying to reason his feelings of death and its justification. Elijah is depressed! His human emotions are running wild within him. Yet, he just ordered the slaughtering of hundreds of the priests of Baal, called fire down from heaven, and consumed an altar filled with false idols. However, the evil spirit behind Jezebel was almost too great for him to deal with and by Jezebel's word she swore death to him before the day's end. This struck a fear in him to the point of wanting to die. Fear is at the heart of people with depression.

God provides.

Spiritual provision is the way the Lord deals with Elijah's depression. In 1 Kings 19:5-8, the Lord sends an angel to feed Elijah. First, with cake and water to give him strength out of his depression. Depression causes such anxiety in a person that they can literally have no physical strength to carry on. Their will has been depleted to the point of no concern. Feeding our physical bodies when feeling depressed is important to rejuvenate the body and restore the soul. And second, God sends an angel to give him meat. This time its for a journey the Lord is commanding him to make. The juniper tree that Elijah slept under during this time was not anywhere near Mt. Horeb which was 180 miles away. It would take Elijah 40 days to reach Mt. Horeb to receive the prophetic word of the Lord. Why would Elijah have to travel 180 miles to the mountain of God just to hear a word that God could have given to him at the Juniper tree?

Depression brings us to a low point in our lives and when God moves on our situation to lift us out that state of despair He will deliver us to the mountaintop. He delivers us to His holy mountain, His inner sanctum, His Holy of Holies to deliver a prophetic word and encourage us to press on. Forty days later Elijah stood before the Lord, just as Israel spent forty days in the wilderness before approaching Mt. Sinai, and Jesus spent forty days in the wilderness before He was tempted. The prophetic word of the Lord came to Elijah and he was commissioned to anoint another as King over Israel; Jehu the son of Nishmi. God changes the government and raises new regimes.

The Lord changes our circumstances and causes blessing to take the place of our depression. He informs us that all is well and many are those of us who serve Him compared to those who have idolized the world. He tells Elijah 7,000 have not bowed their necks to Baal (1 Kings 19:18).

Laziness. Anger is virtually always at the root of laziness. The lazy person most certainly does not comply with a task without complaining. People who engage in this behavior are rebelling against expectations and responsibilities. A spirit of cheat, misuse, and misunderstanding have settled in them and they are afraid to make their own feelings known for fear of punishment or reprisal.

"Laziness casts into a deep sleep, and an idle man will suffer hunger" Proverbs 19:15.

Hypochondria. This is a person who experiences one minor illness or pain after another. Usually the physical discomfort is real, especially in the hypochondriac's mind.

Hypochondria develops in a person when they are made to feel guilty whenever they speak out about something in an assertive manner. They learn to be able to say anything negative, they need to have a good excuse. The illness sets in when they believe this to be the excuse they need to express a legitimate complaint. In fact, their sickness gives them the needed excuse for avoiding people and allowing to them to get away with selfish demands. They control others through their sickness.

"For he who eats and drinks, eats and drinks judgment to himself, if he does not judge the body rightly. For this reason many among you are weak and sick, and a number sleep" 1 Cor. 11:30. Paul proclaims if we do not understand the accomplished efforts of the cross we proclaim a curse upon ourselves. A curse to weakness, sickness, and even death.

Walking through life with a cracked spiritual foundation (not understanding who we are in Christ) can cause harm and a life of discomfort.

"...I will put none of the diseases on you which I have put on the Egyptians (the world); for I, the Lord, am your healer" Ex. 15:26.

Rejection. The effects of silent-passive anger are so deadly because the object of the anger is not given an opportunity to share in working through the problems. Silent anger is specifically designed to kill any type of personal exchange. People who use passive-aggressive behavior are pessimists. They assume that if their true feelings are made known, they will be rejected. Since the anger is not properly dealt with the disadvantages begin to build. It is likely that it will remain inside until a blow-up or an emotional breakdown occurs. They walk in the deception that they have been rejected in all aspects of their life.

The spirit of rejection has a foundation of unbelief at its core. It is an idolatrous spirit and sits in the realm of witchcraft. The truth in this observation rests in the Word of God which clearly expresses God's eternal love for us. *"For God has so loved the world that He gave His only begotten Son..."* John 3:16. *"See how great a love the Father has bestowed on us, that we should be called children of God"* 1 John 3:1. There are over 106 Bible verses in the Scriptures that reference God's love. Yet, the person who walks in rejection has created a system of works in their psyche that will not allow them to believe or understand the revelation of these verses. Why? Because they feel they don't measure up. Instead of walking in grace and believing the Word about His love for them they cannot make the transference from flesh to spirit. A revelation is needed. Revelation comes from the Word of God and the power of the Holy Spirit.

Rejection is a powerful weapon used by the enemy to never allow us to reach the full potential of God's purpose in our lives. If the enemy can keep us in a permanent state of rejection we will operate in life with a tarnished view of everything around us. Our decision-making faculties will be motivated from this point of view. We will walk in a pessimistic view of life. The cup will always be half-empty not half-full.

Resentment. The foundation of resentment is a spirit of jealousy. It is fueled not just by the success of others but also by events in life.

"For jealousy enrages a man, and he will not spare in the day of vengeance" Proverbs 6:34.

Twenty years ago, I confided in a brother in the ministry after he expressed having been discarded by two other ministries he had once regarded as his inner circle. After listening to his story there certainly was no cause for those ministers to brush him aside. He had been a powerful and anointed teacher for them being used at conferences nationally and internationally. They promised a love offering for his ministry and never fulfilled the promise. My desire to confide in him was to show empathy about his situation and to encourage him that the Lord was in control. I confessed to him in confidence that one of those ministries had recently done a similar disservice to me and had broken their word about my attendance at a recent church dedication in the South. Within three weeks I had received a letter from that ministry disfellowshipping me for what they claimed to be insubordination. I was shocked at the disdain of such an occurrence. Never was I called before the elders or the board of that ministry, where I held the prophetic office but I was just presumed guilty of rebellion. I called the Apostle over the ministry and asked for an explanation, especially why I was never able to face my accuser as prescribed in the Scriptures (see Matthew 18:15 and Acts 25:16). The Apostle's answer was vague and judgmental. He told me the brother I had listened to and confided in had broken his confidence and defiled me to the ministry. It was a spirit of jealousy. This brother had continually been seeking to discredit my reputation for many months after that incident. I had already had a twenty year relationship with him. Our ministries are now reconciled but it had taken 15 years to have that happen.

The Apostle in the south who had removed me lost his ministry and has since attached himself to my local church. In fact, I prophesied in his life several times after that incident. The Lord requires we maintain a no judgment zone mentality when it comes to ministry. It is not for us to hold grudges, be jealous of one another or stand in judgment of each other. Forgiveness is the foundation that heals in all situations. It is the key to liberty and releasing the shackles of bondage.

Resentment is a powerful attitude that can cripple relationships in the body of Christ. The Lord is always moving toward reconciliation when a wrong is done. The brother who displayed jealousy toward me, even though we are reconciled, is no longer involved in our church. His jealousy drove him to continue the process of walking around the mountain and not yet attaining the fulfilled call of God in his life. My prayers are continually with him and my fervent prayer is that the Lord fulfill every good thing in his ministry for the sake of the Gospel.

There is no trust or security in resentment. It is a bitter, vile act of desperation. Those who walk with a spirit of resentment are constantly putting others down, so they can raise themselves up above those they resent. It is surrounded in gossip and malicious talk. Resentment divides relationships and plays into the hands of a lying enemy who only looks to destroy. Those who have a spirit of resentment are filled with the conversation of complaints and negativity. They are not happy with any situation unless it involves the 'I' factor (selfishness) drawing attention on them. Self-centeredness is a partner of resentment.

Tyranny. Abusive authority communicates to people its insecurity, and they know in their spirit that they are not strongly loved by a person abusing their authority. When they are cruel and abusive, especially physically, their spirit will respond to the abuser even in the good times with guardedness. The fear of being hurt runs deep, and a battered person cannot rest comfortably in a relationship shadowed by unpredictability. The damage done by their anger leaves the relationship irreparable, even after they find help to reverse their destructive patterns.

People who are tyrannical operate not from godly concern for the relationship's welfare but from fear of the criticism. A person's tyrannical behavior indicates insecurity not strength. The victim instinctively knows this, yet they accommodate the insecure abuse out of emasculating pity toward the tyranny. This type of behavior indicates a dysfunction of cruelty and a false sense of protection against the victim. They cannot get close in the relationship or any relationship.

A tyrannical spirit is evident to those they are in relationship with, regardless of their behavior or words. Though they may not be able to verbalize it, they know when the tyranny is being exercised with wrong authority. They know when it is being used for self-protection rather than initiating strong and loving leadership with everyone's good in mind. When we lord our spirit over those under our authority we have created a tyrannical situation. It reminds me of the proverbial saying, "My way or the highway." There is no room for compromise. This behavior immediately dismisses any discussion on the subject shutting down the lines of communication and telling the person that it is done to that they do not matter AT ALL! It's all about ME! Either you're for me or you're against me. No gray areas, black and white situations only.

CONTROL, CONTROL, and more CONTROL! The person with a tyrannical spirit is saying, "I don't trust you!" "My way is the best way." "There's no room for discussion!" and the very popular dismissive phrase, "GET OVER IT!"

7

The Lies We Believe

"Good thoughts bear good fruit, bad thoughts bad fruit"-
Dr. James Allen

The spiritual principle of seed faith governs the Christian world — that thoughts bear after their own kind — is one of the truest messages of personal hope. It makes emotional well-being available to anyone who is willing to dedicate himself to knowing, believing, and practicing truth.

"For as a man reckons in his soul, so he is" Proverbs 23:7.

If the message placed in us most of our lives is recorded negativity and a barrage of verbal garbage that we will never measure up to immeasurable unattainable fantasy standards then our outcome is a life of low self-esteem. We will never fulfill the God-given destiny in our lives and we will become settlers not sojourners. Our programming will be downloaded to a mediocre existence. No confidence, a system of works not grace, no room for failure, and many other dysfunctions will become the mantra for living. It will affect our decision-making process, the choices we choose through life, and the passive-aggressive persona that this is all there ever will be.

Negative Power Statements.

"I must have everyone's love and approval." -- This statement is based on a life operating in a system of works. There is no room for mistakes and the person living in it develops a perfectionist mentality. If we don't measure up how can anyone ever love us? How can God love me? "Unless everyone loves and accepts me, I can't feel good about myself." These power statements are a re-sounding alarm going off in the person's head with low self-esteem on a consistent basis. This is the lie they essentially believe. This lie puts your emotional well-being into the hands of people who may not be trustworthy. It gives sizable power to others over you. It opens you up to be taken advantage of and manipulated.

  The emotional fall-out of this conflict is that we bounce back and forth between guilt and anger. Anger or guilt. Not such a great choice. The truth is that some people aren't going to like us or what we do, no matter how hard we try. In the attempt to gain everyone's love and approval through chronic acquiescence we can lose ourselves. The way to keep ourselves from this lie is to tell ourselves the truth, "you can't have everyone's approval and that's okay." If we will get this statement into our spirit then the lie will wane in scope of this practice. You will consciously hear the truth and get your emotions under control to make a reasoned decision.

"My unhappiness is somebody else's fault." — Our way of thinking about life's events is what makes or breaks us emotionally. This lie takes that ideal one unhealthy step further. It allows me to pass the buck for all my emotional upsets onto somebody else. It points a finger outward. No responsibility taken here. "It's all your fault that I'm angry." Picture yourself

in a long line at the grocery store. It is not moving. You are getting angrier by the minute, stamping your foot, looking at the time on your cellphone. The lady at the register is fumbling around in her purse to count out pennies for exact change. Ask yourself: Is it really the lady counting out her pennies taking her time that is upsetting me or is it the way I am approaching the event in my mind?

The emotional reactions of people concerning certain events are usually motivated through similar circumstances, such as, the death of a loved one. Those involved share the same belief system; death is sad causing a similar reaction of grief. However, when we change the scenario to a suffering loved one going home to be with the Lord, as Christians, our belief system secures a different reaction and our values are based on the Word of God. We are saddened that the sufferer has gone home to be with the Lord, yet relieved and filled with joy for their eternal life. We know they are heaven bound because of their faith in Christ. To the unsaved in this same scenario their emotional system is filled with doubt about an uncertain eternity. They know death is inevitable but they cannot walk in the joy of our spiritual certainty concerning eternal life. Two different emotions based on one having Christ and the other without Jesus in their lives.

Having Jesus in your life should make all the difference concerning your emotional reaction when standing in that line that is not moving as fast as you'd like it to. Just as having Christ makes the difference because of our belief system when a loved one dies. If you have Christ, yet, are still feeling emotions of anger and impatience arising when in long lines that are delayed, there is a dysfunctional system of works operating in you. It needs to re-programmed. Your focus needs to be on the Word of God and His instructions to you when in these situations.

An Exercise that brings change. Consider situations in life to be like two circles; a circle in a circle. There is a larger circle that is everyday life. You participate in it and live and dwell in it. It is a part of you. In that larger circle you cannot control the events that occur. For example; the weather is a daily occurrence in your larger circle. You cannot control the weather, yet it is a part of your daily life. You can prepare for the weather, if it's raining you can dress appropriately and bring along an umbrella to deal with the rain. If it's snowing, windy and cold, you can dress accordingly, and so on and so forth. You just can't change the outcome of the elements of the weather patterns you encounter in that larger circle of your daily life. Now vision the smaller second circle. It sits inside the larger circle of your life. You can control what is taking place within that smaller circle. It is your decision-making process. Your attitudes, your choices, your emotions, they are all wrapped up in that smaller circle. In dealing with the weather you can't change the rain or snow from falling but you can approach it with a positive attitude and make the choice to not let it get you down. Your choices in that smaller circle in dealing with the weather was the preparations you made to be prepared to confront the weather system accordingly.

In that long line where the lady in front of you is fumbling around for her exact change (the larger circle) and (the smaller circle; the one where you can choose to control your feelings) as you are feeling the rise of emotional impatience, you can choose not to be and you can exercise God's Word in your life to be loving, kind, and patient with one another just as the Lord is patient with you. It is clearly a choice of horizontal vision versus vertical vision. I can look horizontally on what is happening around me and allow my emotions to entertain impatience or I can look vertically keeping my eyes on Jesus and allow my emotions to be controlled by the Spirit which is in me. Ask yourself, which is the greater witness?

I worked for many years in corporate America as a Regional Manager of Sales for a German company. Decisions are made by the Board of Directors, the CEO, and other top executives in that company quarterly and then the vision is presented along with their decisions in making the vision become a reality to the mid-level executives. It is our responsibility, as mid-level managers, to carry out the decisions made at the top executive level. In my tenth year with the company they made the decision to eliminate my Regional executive position. It didn't matter that I was always in the top three of all managers as a profitable producer of the company's bottom line. The decision was made (the larger circle). I could not control nor change that decision. I was out and looking for work. However, what I could control was how I dealt with that decision (the smaller circle). I could have let depression set in or anger or any of the horizontal emotions that the world places in front of us daily or I could approach it with a positive attitude (God's attitude) knowing that God has my back and that He is my provider and strong tower. I would choose to handle the situation with the Word of God. In that choice lies the victory over my unfortunate. circumstances.

Low self-esteem is the emotional enemy of our soul and it sets in motion high-mindedness when dealing with circumstances beyond our control. It is a faulty foundation and a distorted belief system. A system of works. It is a dysfunctional belief system of defense that creates a false security emotionally. This causes us to make wrong decisions and at times brings our emotions to uncontrollable levels. Our emotional stability must rest in the Word of God.

"I am only as good as what I do." — This is a foundational statement of a system of works. It is a powerful motivation that stirs our emotions to make decisions that we justify as being God's will, yet those decisions are clearly made from a dysfunctional belief. It is never God's will to make decisions based on this dysfunction. This type of thinking clouds our judgments and causes us to make decisions that are not healthy to our well-being.

Somehow along the way we have gotten our character and integrity mixed up with externals. Top sales representative in a company translates to him being a great man. We know this not to be true. This attitude may be an inescapable part of our competitive living, it has created a feeling in many of us that we are only as good as our last performance. Perfectionists equate their self-worth with performance which creates an internal pressure that can't be handled. Talent and ability felled by lies is a pressure cooker waiting to explode.

Even though our performances in life do say something about us they are never complete representations of who we are. A person's income level is never a statement about their value as a child of God. It is also not a litmus test for God's favor. This is a difficult lie to overcome. What then should be the basis of self-esteem? The answer to this question is that it truly comes from our Creator and not what we do or how we perform. We need to view ourselves in vertical dimensions — seeing who we are in Christ's eyes, not the horizontal dimension of doing all we can to impress others through achievement or success. The Lord sees us as being wonderfully made (Ps. 139) and valuable to the purchasing of our souls with the life of His Son (Jn. 3:16).

God sees us as having great worth because He created us in His image (Gen. 2). This is the true basis for self-esteem.

It's in the living of this truth that the difficulty comes. We live in a world system that is predicated on performance not who we are in Christ. Solomon himself was acutely aware of this truth. All his riches, all his wives, all his authority, and all his wisdom he writes is futile in the universal understanding of who God is and all that God represents. Jesus presented this principle to His disciples after Peter's confession of Him being the Christ. *"For what does it profit a man to gain the whole world, and forfeit his soul?"* Mark 8:36.

"Life should be fair." –Fairness is taught in our homes, our schoolyards, and through our political system. The goodness in this statement is that it develops our character and shows we are cared for and loved equally, especially in our homes. However, the downside to this statement is that it fosters a belief that life would always be fair which it definitely is not!

This life is fair syndrome is a lie that is just as pervasive as it is potent. It's wishful thinking and it is damaging. Solomon understood this principle of life when he penned in Ecclesiastes 8:14, *"There is futility which is done on the earth, that is, there are righteous men to whom it happens according to the deeds of the wicked. On the other hand, there are evil men to who it happens according to the deeds of the righteous. I say this too is futility."*

Of course, life isn't always fair. Saying so would be a big lie. The spark of the divine in us all often wants to play fair and expect others to do the same. It is our expectation that is the problem. People who are driven by this lie, who harbor decades of resentment, have only one resource to become emotionally well. They must strike a balance for healthy truth.

We need to engage in Jesus-talk. The Word of God is the key to balance in these matters of unfairness. The need for Jesus-talk keeps the past and the present separate. It helps us to step out of the victim's role and cope with current realities. It's up to us to handle unfairness so as not to pay for it twice — once when it happened and once when we allow it to wreck our lives presently.

"Black and White." –If you've ever had this criticism launched your way, you are being accused of a style of distorted thinking called polarization. Polarization cuts reality into two fabrics of life—the all or nothing at all—black and white extremes.

If you polarize, you often find yourself reacting to things with either a "that was great!" statement or "oh, that was awful!" This style of thinking does not allow you to see the greys in life, much less appreciate them. If turned inward, polarization thinking brings severe emotional fallout.

One of the more serious inward forms of polarization thinking is **the 'sinner/saint' syndrome**. We either see ourselves as completely sinful or completely saint-like flipping back and forth between the two. We distort reality when we see only the extremes in ourselves and others. This causes us to miss seeing the whole person.

The "saints" are an interesting group. People in their wildest dreams never thought they'd be doing the things they can do. The truth about themselves is that they can do almost anything. The "saints" do not—cannot—believe this truth. When they "fall," they simply are in shock about the "impossibility" of their actions. Usually it takes a tremendous amount of work to help such people see the arrogance behind their assumption that they are too good to do such things.

There are certain black-and-white issues and we need to view them that way. The existence of God is a black-and-white issue. He either exists or he doesn't. Jesus Christ was either the Son of God (God Incarnate) or he was not. Sins against society such as murder or stealing are also black-and-white issues.

The polarized thinker takes all of life and forces it into a black-and-white format. Unfortunately, when the issues are grey, as many are, polarized thinking creates needless anger and hurt. We need to be more accurate in judging and discerning issues of shaded areas of life.

"All my problems are caused by my sins." — This is the Job factor. People have been hearing and believing that problems are caused by sin alone. Logic holds no sway with this lie, which is the "God messes up our lives to punish us for our sins" lie. As humans we like to explain things. We like to explain the universe to one another, to have a grasp of the future. Everything must be for a reason, we can control the future in some way. Believing we are the cause of all our problems is an easy lie to believe. If this were true, all we'd have to do is stay out of trouble. But we cannot always be good and when we believe this lie on top that inevitability, we doom ourselves to a guilt-ridden life we wouldn't wish on anyone.

There is sin we commit that can be the source of our problems such as stealing, lying, and other actions such as these. There is also sin committed that is the result of another person's actions and we are somehow attached to that person. For example, a business partner who embezzles funds. But then there are problems resulting from no sin at all. A house fire, lightning strikes, and tornados or hurricanes hitting our homes causing tremendous damage are no fault of ours and certainly not caused by our sin. We must look at this truth from the eyes of the Lord. The blind man at the gate was blind from birth so that the Son of Man may be glorified. It had nothing to do with his parents sin or his sin. There are times God will allow bad things to happen in our lives that He may be glorified and lifted for the salvation of men's souls (John 9:1). He allows it to happen in our lives that we may mature in the character of Jesus Christ. He allows it to happen in our lives that we will be promoted into deeper prosperity in Him.

The challenge is to honestly examine the root of a given problem. It the root is personal sin, then that sin does need to be dealt with before the problem can be solved. If the problem is at the hand of another, then we need not allow any condemnation to fall upon us so as to spend the rest of our lives feeling guilty over something we did not cause, all because of a lie.

"Depression, anger, and anxiety are signs of a weak faith in God."

The belief that we shouldn't feel what we feel often results in 'repression.' Repression is taking what you feel and suppressing it so that you don't feel it. But the feelings never really go away. They stay buried in the subconscious ready to come out when we tire of the effort expended to keep them repressed. Ultimately, when too many feelings get 'repressed,' the result is a volcanic reaction to the logjam of emotions — never happening at the most convenient times. Playing "the Christians never get angry or depressed" tape long enough can backfire on you.

"Don't get depressed, God hasn't forgotten you." "It must be God's will, so everything will work out." And, "If you trust in God, you can 'in everything give thanks.'"

These are true statements. However, God didn't just give us pleasurable feelings. We got the whole gamut of emotions, from pain to pleasure. So, if He gave us so many ways to feel, why would He want us to only experience the positive ones? Tell yourself the depression state when hurting is normal. Grieve through it and move on. Just don't carry it around the rest of your life. Jesus expressed some pretty strong emotions; He wept at the death of Lazarus and over Jerusalem, He got angry in the Temple, turning over the money-changer tables, and He had some harsh words for the Pharisees.

There are times, though, that anger, anxiety, and depression can very will indicate a lack of faith in God and who He is. Strong emotions that show up frequently should make us question what's happening to us. Emotions that are overwhelming intense can also be a sign our faith needs tending. If I lose my job and become so intensely depressed that I cannot function, perhaps I do not strongly believe in God's ability to help me handle problems. Also, strong, painful emotions that last a long time can signal a problem with faith in God's ability to run the universe. When this happens it is safe to say that this person's faith is weak. So weak that they cannot forgive or forget—which God commands us to do in no uncertain terms, *"...forgive me Lord, as I have forgiven them..."* the Lord's Prayer.

We need to ourselves permission to feel what we feel, and at the same time we must be honest enough to examine whether or not the feeling fits what has happened to us. Neither "volcanic" or "repression" feelings can help us. Seeking the middle ground on what we feel and express is the acceptance we need to give ourselves to help us move on.

Learn to replace lies with truth.

If we accept the Bible as God's Word, we have a guide for truth in life. *"All Scripture is given by inspiration by God, and is profitable for doctrine, for reproof, for correction, for instruction in righteousness, that the man of God may be complete, thoroughly equipped for every good work"* 2 Timothy 3:16-17.

The truth of the Scriptures needs to become the guide to understanding all other truth from God's perspective. The Bible is the most direct way to seek God's truth. Let Scriptural truth become the prerequisite for health; physically (body), emotionally (soul), and spiritually (Spirit). We must seek truth and live by what is true because what we see as truth is what primarily determines our path through life.

"For truth is reality. That which is false is unreal. The more clearly, we see the reality of the world, the better equipped we are to deal with the world. The less clearly we see the reality of the world – the more our minds are befuddled by falsehood, misperceptions, and illusions – the less able we sill be to determine correct courses of action and make wise decisions. Our view of reality is like a map...If the map is true and accurate, we will generally know how to get there. If the map is false and inaccurate, we generally will be lost.

-Dr. Scott Peck, Road, 44.

There is another important reason why we must seek the truth and live by it. There is a direct, inescapable connection between our self-esteem and whether we are dedicated to truth. If dedication to truth characterizes our way of living, we develop stable positive feelings of worth. The moment we wrap our lives around lies, genuine feelings of self-worth are virtually impossible. We've all had moments in our lives when we suddenly saw that something we believed to be true was false. Instantly, the truth cuts like a knife. *"As a man thinks in his heart, so is he"* Proverbs 23:7.

8

A Secret Society

"Would not God find this out? For He knows the secrets of the heart" Psalm 44:21.

There are numerous aspects of man that are known to God. Each of these aspects manifests the sinfulness and evil intent of men's hearts. Our flesh betrays us in a secret society.

- **Man's imaginations.** *"Then it shall come about, when many evils and troubles have come upon them, that this song will testify before them as a witness...for I know their intent which they are developing today..."* Deut. 31:21.
- **The hearts of men.** *"...for God sees not as man sees, for man looks at the outward appearance, but the Lord looks at the heart"* 1 Samuel 16:7.
- **All the ways of man.** *"For the Lord knows the way of the righteous, But the way of the wicked will perish'* Psalm 1:6.
- **The secrets of the heart.** *"For He knows the secrets of the heart"* Psalm 44:21.
- **The thoughts of men.** *"The Lord knows the thoughts of men"* Psalm 94:11.
- **The thoughts of man afar off.** *"...Thou dost understand my thought from afar"* Psalm 139:2.
- **Every word in the tongue.** *"Even before there is a word on my tongue, Behold, O Lord, Thou dost know it all"* Psalm 139:4.

- **Works and thoughts of man.** *"For I know their works and their thoughts..."* Isaiah 66:18.
- **The thoughts and intents of the heart.** *"For the word of God is living and active and sharper than any two-edged sword and piercing as far as the division of soul and spirit, of both joints and marrow, and able to judge the thoughts and intentions of the heart"* Hebrews 4:12.
- **The deceitfulness of the heart.** *"The heart is more deceitful than all else and is desperately sick; who can understand it?"* Jeremiah 17:9 and *"Your eyes will see strange things, and your heart will utter perverse things"* Proverbs 23:33.

The heart betrays who we have been designed to be in Christ. It harbors chambers of resentment, bitterness, and revenge. It keeps a secret chamber of deceitfulness and lies. It is only in surrendering to Christ that the heart becomes like Him. Yet, the battle still rages even after the surrender. Our heart before Christ has been the place where the flesh nature in man has set its throne. It has harbored the darkness and battles to keep our heart in this realm.

John 1:4-5, *"In Him was life; and the life was the light of men. And the light shines in the darkness; and the darkness did not [overpower] it."* Jesus came to shed light and the darkness did not comprehend it. This aspect of the work of Christ performed and accomplished the salvation of men and saved us from the evil intent of our hearts.

Generational curses, our flesh nature, and the hurtful ways in us have a set the courses of low self-esteem, high-mindedness, arrogance, deception, and lies in our lives using these building blocks upon a foundation of human feelings and emotions that betray the very nature of Christ in us. There is no good in man except Jesus Christ and Him crucified. If men do not walk in the freedom of the work of Christ, they have no hope of the accomplished working power of salvation through the cross.

The person who suffers from low self-esteem issues exposed through uncontrolled anger, resentment, projectionism, and the like are deceived in thinking they can obtain the full blessing of God's desire for their lives without having these ungodly roots plucked from their hearts. The battle rages in them and one great weapon of the evil heart is to keep a secret place and surround the person in a life of secrecy. In that thinking, they are deceived! The deception is the veil that the flesh masks while the victim of this atrocity of the heart is drowning in a system of worldly works. They are on a merry-go-round of emotions never attaining the peace that God so dearly has bestowed upon them. They need deliverance.

I counseled a ministry leader who at first glance seems to have everything most people called to ministry would desire. He has over 46 churches under his apostleship, broadcasts several different Christian television programs, is a sought after national and international speaker, ministers in dozens of churches yearly, sends out a newsletter with a huge following, is on twitter, Facebook, ministers at conventions, and is in demand at many other very large international ministries of well-known God's generals in the kingdom. **The gifts of the Spirit** (1 Cor. 12 and Eph. 4) are evident in him. The problem is he lacks **the fruit of the Spirit.** The gifts were given to him when he accepted Christ and received the Holy Spirit however the fruit of the Spirit which is the love of God has not manifested itself in him because he still harbors sinfulness in his heart. He is an angry man. His anger is harbored in the secret place of his heart and is only known to his wife and family. They are the recipients of this evil and the suffering they are enduring has manifested itself. God is shedding light on his personality disorders.

In him is a hurtfulness that has been seeded years early from childhood. It was never dealt with and replaced with the understanding of God's love for him. He has surrounded himself with a defense mechanism of false theology quoting God's word to justify his bad behavior. His family has become enablers in this process keeping his explosive anger a secret. The reason for his call was to try to understand why his THIRD wife just left him.

Most times the emotional pain that is associated with low self-esteem is so hurtful that we condition ourselves to create a defense mechanism to justify our dysfunctional actions. Keeping things secret is a major part of that deception. This minister is well liked in his ministry circles because no one knows the dark secret he harbors in his heart that is resurrected in his home life in the form of anger and verbal abuse. He has trained himself emotionally to show a loving demeanor to his ministry partners, yet the partner God gave him in life suffers; his wife.

When his sin was exposed, he immediately went into protection mode. He created falsehoods about those who are the victims of his vial tirades. He has demeaned his wife's character to others claiming she is bipolar and has psychological issues. He refuses to take responsibility for his verbal abuse and occasional physical abuse toward his wife. The evil in his heart has gone on full alert to protect his actions of deceit rather than allowing the healing power of God to show him a better way and release him from his tormented life. When he receives counsel on how to get to the root cause of this issue of anger, he defames the counselor's reputation and character rather than deal with his own dysfunction. His hurt and dysfunction is so great that he cannot see it because of the deceitfulness of his heart. He needs deliverance.

The secret places of the heart become vital in our refusal to deal with the sinfulness in it. When the sin manifests itself in the form of sexual lust, lying, gossip, and the nature of the flesh as Paul describes in Galatians 5:19-21, secrecy becomes an important tool in that process. Even when God sheds light on the dark places of the heart revealing our sinfulness the nature of the flesh fights to keep it secret.

"For nothing is hidden, except to be revealed; not has anything been secret, but that it should come to light" Mark 4:22.

The Greek word describes the secrecy of the heart as **krupto**. It is translated *'to hide.'* *"And after these things Joseph of Arimathea, being a disciple of Jesus, but a [krupto] secret one, for fear of the Jews..."* John 19:38. The intention theologically in this word is to keep hidden because of fear. The secret places of the heart with evil intent are just that . Kept there because of fear. If we harbor evil in our hearts and through secrecy keep them protected and preserved, it is the fear of exposure that motivates this process. It is a trust issue. We don't trust God to love us through the process of healing, we don't trust that we can love ourselves through the process without the burden of guilt and condemnation, and we don't trust others to give us the mercy and grace to get through the healing process for fear we will be judged.

However, the Lord desires to set us free. His reason for exposing what is hidden in the secret places of the heart is to fulfill in us the loving character of Jesus Christ and set us free from the bondage we have allowed to remain in our lives.

The minister who has the anger issue and only reveals it with his family but keeps it secret to ministry contacts will not reach the full potential of ministry that God has designed for him until he deals with the anger issue in his life. The Lord has great plans for him to become the next general of the kingdom. However, he will not get there without allowing his character to become more like Christ. It is not the gifting of the Spirit that God is concerned with but rather the fruit of the Spirit in him which is love [agapeo]. The Lord will continue to tug at his heart and work on his character until the day of completion to rid him and his family of the anger in him. Then he will see the true freedom God has bestowed upon him through the working power of the Holy Spirit. He must clear out his secret place of the heart's evil intentions.

It's a Society

The heart harbors many evil's that create a society of secrecy and dysfunction. The society has many members such as anger, low self-esteem, high-mindedness, projectionism, sexual dysfunctions, lust, lying, deceitfulness, adultery, pornography, and the like. It causes the person with these issues to become proficient in the blame game, finger pointing, transference of responsibilities, unforgiveness, rejections, and many more.

The person with secrecy in their life will work harder at keeping those evil intensions secret than they will at resolving them and covering them in the blood of Jesus Christ which would bring about healing and freedom from their bondage. They are willing to pay the dues owed to this society rather than come to the revelation that Jesus Christ has already paid the price for their righteousness. Make no mistake, the dues are expensive, and many have paid with multiple divorces, estranged relationships, rejected ministries, and intimacy issues.

The secret society convinces the holder of this membership to believe it is easier to maintain the charade rather than deal with the sin. Therefore, a revelation is needed to set the person free. They are not convinced they are in any danger emotionally that is the reason for needed revelation. Revelation requires revealed truth and truth is painful. Most of us don't like to hear the truth about ourselves and will sometimes react with hurt, even anger, when we do. Also, truth is sometimes painful because it forces us to give up lies that we may have grown accustomed to or with which we feel secure. Giving up what makes us feel secure — even if it's miserable security — is hard.

Telling the truth about a situation even about ourselves could cost us hardship and pain. We can suffer in our personal and professional lives because of it. Yet, the truth about ourselves and our personal lives can potentially be packed with pain and upheaval before it leads us to emotional health. We need resolve and awareness to get through the pain to the truth. Many of us need to rip up the foundation of emotional doubt, anxiety, fear, and low self-esteem so that the Lord may rebuild the temple in us. God wants to set us on a firm foundation with a house built on the rock not sand. In an earlier chapter I referenced Matthew 7:24-27. It is the teaching by Jesus on the two foundations. One built on the rock and the other on the sand. The hardships of life are the same for both foundations; rain, wind, and floods coming against them. Yet the results are quite different. The foundation on the rock stands strong against these adversities. The foundation built on sand falls and great is its fall.

Each foundation faces the same storms, but the manifestation of the fruit is very different. The rock produces joy, love, peace, harmony, praise and worship, and a life filled with the fruit of the Spirit wrapped in God's grace. The sand produces quite a different result. It is founded on a system of works and its fruit is of the flesh. Its deeds display *immorality, impurity, sensuality, idolatry, sorcery, enmities, strife, jealousy, outbursts of anger, disputes, dissensions, factions, envyings, drunkenness, carousings, and things like these,"* (Gal. 5:19-21) of which Paul forewarns us in Galatians 5:21, *"that those who practice such things shall not inherit the kingdom of God."*

In the beginning of this chapter on page 104, I list several members of the secret society of the evil intents of our heart. Each one of these members carries the enemies mark. It is satanic fellowship when we entertain these evils in our lives. These societal members are steeped in witchcraft with the sole purpose to deceive you in this life and keep you from the kingdom. They are not necessarily salvation issues although they ultimately can be. They are certainly emotional issues that will prevent you from God's blessings and prevent you from reaching your fullest potential in Christ.

"...the Lord will bring to light the things hidden in the darkness and disclose the motives of men's hearts..." 1 Corinthians 4:5.

How can we fulfill the will of God in our lives if we are not willing to work out our salvation in fear **[respect]** and trembling **[humility]** (Phil. 2:12) in the presence of an awesome, powerful, and righteous God? Or do you not know that the ***"anger of man does not achieve the righteousness of God?"*** James 1:20. The meaning behind Philippians 2:12, *fear and trembling or respect and humility,* is two-fold. First, the Greek verb rendered 'workout' means to continually work to bring to completion or fruition. We do this by actively pursuing obedience in the process of sanctification, which Paul explains further in the Philippian text (see Philippians 3; the goal of life). He describes himself as 'straining' and 'pressing on' toward a goal of Christlikeness. *"Brethren, I do not regard myself as having laid hold of it yet; but one thing I do: forgetting what lies behind and reaching forward to what lies ahead, I press on toward the goal for the prize of the upward call of God in Christ Jesus"* Philippians 3:13-14.

Second, 'trembling' can also refer to a shaking due to weakness, but this is a weakness of higher purpose, one which brings us to a state of dependency on God. Obedience and submission to the God we revere, and respect is our 'reasonable service' (Romans 12:1-2) and brings great joy. Psalm 2:11 sums it up perfectly: *"Serve the Lord with fear and rejoice with trembling."* We work out our salvation by going to the very source of our salvation — the Word of God, surrender to Jesus Christ His Son, and sealed in the Holy Spirit of Promise — wherein we renew our hearts and minds (Romans 12:1-2), coming into His presence with a Spirit of reverence and awe. In this process there is no room for a secret society. It must be exposed for the work to come to full fruition; Christlikeness.

"The things you have learned and received and heard and seen in me, practice these things; and the God of peace shall be with you"
Philippians 4:9.

Lies and Deception

Lying and deception are the foundation of a secret society. Just as apostles and prophets are the cornerstone of the church in righteousness so lying and deception are the cornerstone of the deeds of the flesh.

Liars are willing to bear false witness against their brothers, their ministries, their churches, or any other entity that presents a roadblock to the truth. These are the things that prevent healing and emotional stability from giving them a healthy disposition.

An Exciting Truth can be Eclipsed by a Thrilling Lie!

Many of the lies we will not doubt are the ones we want desperately to be true. Some lies just sound better than the truth. The motivating factor to this type of lying is nested in low self-esteem. We want people's approval and if only for a moment of that pat on the back, we will lie to get it. A televangelist posted and tweeted on his website how his ministry had brought about the salvation of over 1.6 million souls due to his preaching broadcasts on a certain television network. Well, Hallelujah! Right? Who wouldn't say well done good and faithful servant and brother in Christ? There is only one problem. He was a participant in the programming of these telecasts not the keynote speaker as his webcasts and tweets would have led us to believe. There were several other ministers who preached on this project that resulted in 1.6 million souls being saved. Some might say that is semantics. Not so, it's deception! A lying spirit! A witchcraft spirit to deceive his donors into thinking his ministry is more than it really is. To this televangelist, perception is the motivation behind the deception. He is telling us that he has been the sole factor in this event. In truth, it was the preaching of several televangelists.

An exciting truth, but a more thrilling lie. It is the lack of Christlikeness in this televangelist that would cause him to deceive everyone into thinking it was his ministry's effort that brought these salvations about. If he had the integrity and character of Christ in him, it would have been no issue to give credit to all involved and not mislead others into thinking his ministry is something it is not. He even allowed an international televangelist to reap accolades on his webcam telecast deceiving him and his followers into thinking something that was not. However, to him the results justify the means. **Lies and deception are the work of the devil**. They never have any place in the work of the kingdom of God.

Thrilling lies are a tool of the world spawned by the devil. He was there in the Garden at the beginning to present it to Eve, he was prophesied about in Isaiah 14 trying to raise his throne above the Most-High God, and he is called **'the father of lies'** by Christ. *"You are of your father the devil, and you want to do the desires of your father. He was a murderer from the beginning, and does not stand in the truth, because there is no truth in him. Whenever he speaks a lie, he speaks from his own nature; for he is a liar, and the father of lies"* John 8:44. If we participate in lies with a lying spirit, we are in fellowship with the father of lies and that lying spirit.

There is hope when standing against the secret society in the evil intent of men's hearts. It is to stand in the truth of God's Word. To combat the lies, truth must be presented. We must face the truth of God's Word in all respects for God brings truth to us only in love [agapeo].

"If you abide in My word, then you are truly disciples of Mine; and you shall know the truth, and the truth shall make you free"
John 8:31-32.

9

The Power of Confession*

*(This chapter inserted from "Stepping Into Greatness)

*"...if you **confess** with your mouth Jesus as Lord, and believe in your heart that God raised Him from the dead, you shall be saved" Romans 10:9*

Confession is a power action word. It requires the conscious decision to believe God's Word. The decision to do this from the heart results in righteousness. The act of confession involves a process in which to hear the Word of God. *"So, faith comes from hearing, and hearing by the word of Christ"* Romans 10:17.

Confession and faith

There are four foundational principles in the act of confession leading to faith.

(1) **Confession with the mouth**. This action acknowledges Jesus Christ as having been confessed before men and in doing so He confesses us before the Father (Matt. 10:32).

(2) **Believing from the heart**. It is in believing that righteousness is established. Abraham believed God that he would have an heir and it was reckoned to him as righteousness (Romans 4:3).

(3) **Hearing the Word of God.** When the Word of God is preached and in that preaching those who hear it are present it establishes the power of faith (Romans 10:17).

(4) **Faith in His promises.** *"And without faith it is impossible to please Him, for he who comes to God must believe that He is, and that He is a rewarder of those who seek Him"* Hebrews 11:6. Our spiritual father, Abraham, did not see all the promises of God fulfilled in his lifetime. However, that did not stop him from believing in their eventual fulfillment in Christ Jesus. He walked in those promises as though they already were complete.

Confession establishes relationship

When a covenant was established between God and Abraham in Genesis 17 there was an exchange of names as prescribed in covenantal law; *"No longer shall your name be called Abram, but your name shall be Abraham"* Genesis 17:5. 68 The latter part of Abram-*'ham'* added to his name is a derivative of God's name; Jehovah. God adding His name to Abram resulting in Abraham. In this ritual the names are openly pronounced to each other and a covenant relationship is developed. In the same way when we confess Christ as our Lord and Savior His name is added to ours and ours to His in-covenant relationship.

This is only one of many benefits that bestowed upon us when we enter the everlasting covenant of Jesus Christ. With this covenant comes privilege and power. We can boldly enter the Holy of Holies and commune with the Father because the name of Jesus is with us. We can ask anything in His name and it will be given to us. *"And whatever you ask in My name, that will I do that the Father may be glorified in the Son.*

If you ask Me anything in My name, I will do it" John 14:13-14. We can take authority over the dominions of this fallen world, all its principalities and powers, declare healing to the sick, and prosperity to the destitute. *"Truly, truly, I say to you, he who believes in Me, the works that I do shall he do also; and greater works than these shall he do; because I go to the Father"* John 14:12.

The reasons for greater works

The establishment of the New Covenant and its benefits are based upon better promises and confirmed by greater powers because the fullness of grace is now possible in Christ through His Holy Spirit. The following are some examples of the reasons for this greater power to bring about greater works.

- **Satan has been defeated.** On the cross Jesus proclaimed, *"It is finished!"* He has beaten the prince of darkness and every fallen angel. The demonic horde has been defeated (Rev. 20:2).
- **The power of the cross.** Our redemption has been made complete by the Lamb of God who sacrificed Himself upon the tree at Calvary. His shed blood satisfied God that the price was paid for the sin of mankind that was inherited and birthed into our flesh nature in the Garden (Joshua 3:16, the waters pushed back to cross the Jordan River a symbol of the salvation of Israel to enter the Promised Land all the way to ADAM).
- **The baptism of the Holy Spirit (Pentecost).** With the glorification of Christ and His ascension to the throne He sent us His Holy Spirit. In doing so all the rights, powers, anointing, glory, and holiness of the Father

was bestowed upon us. We have been given Christ authority (Acts 1:4-8; 2:33).

- **Time to receive all the gifts of the Holy Spirit.** Pentecost was the defining moment in the life of the Christian church to receive all the gifts and the fruit of the Spirit, which we could only receive in part in the Old Covenant (John 14:16-17).
- **All authority given to Christ.** *"Therefore also God highly exalted Him, and bestowed on Him the name which is above every name, that at the name of Jesus every knee should bow, of those who are in heaven, and on earth, and under the earth, and that every tongue should confess that Jesus Christ is Lord, to the glory of God the Father"* Philippians 2:9-11. He has been given headship over all powers, dominions, and principalities. The authority given to Him He has given to us (John 14:12-14).
- **No limitations in Christ.** We have received the full benefits of the Gospel through the cross of Jesus Christ and are now sealed in the Holy Spirit of Promise (2 Cor. 1:20).
- **Entrance into the Holy of Holies.** We have gained the right to enter boldly before the throne of Grace because of Jesus Christ. We gain access to the most holy place in all creation; the Holiest of All! We can make our requests known and ask of the Father so that He may will it according to His good pleasure (Hebrews 4:16).

Casting no shadow of doubt

Doubting that God will do what He has promised in His Word is a lack of faith and this attitude should not be in any Christian. There is no time for it and heaven has no tolerance to it. In fact, the world needs to witness the greatness of the God we serve and the results of Jesus as our overcomer. When applying this to prophecy in our lives the same principle is in play. Doubt will delay the prophetic word given to you. In 1992 I was ministering at a Full Gospel Businessmen's breakfast in Westfield, MA. The Lord spoke to me in the spirit about a young woman who was going to attend the meeting. I did not know who she was at this point I had never met her. The Lord did show me why she was going to ask for prayer. As I began the altar call for prayer, she stepped forward seeking deliverance from cigarette smoking. She said she lost her deliverance after some Christians prayed for her three weeks earlier at another meeting. God began to give me a **word of knowledge** (1 Cor. 12) about her situation and why she smoked in the first place. I asked her when she started and the circumstances surrounding the start of that habit. She proceeded to explain that her mom forbids her to smoke cigarettes at the age of 14. So, in rebellion to her mom's instruction she grabbed cigarettes from her mom's purse in defiance to mom's wish. God told me to let her know that rebellion was the issue not a needed deliverance from what she called a spirit of nicotine as the other Christian ministry had told her. The Lord instructed me to tell her to go to her mom and ask forgiveness for this blatant act of rebellion and if she did God would deliver her from the desire to pick up and smoke any cigarettes. Several months later I was coming down the runway ramp at Bradley International Airport when this woman ran calling my name. She had an airline uniform on and I had thought maybe I forgot some luggage on the airplane. When she approached me, she asked if I'd remembered her? I did not. So, she began to reiterate the story. When she approached her mom for forgiveness the Holy Spirit leaped inside her and instantly delivered her from any desire to smoke. She had been free from smoking for over six months at that time.

There was no doubt in me that God wanted to touch her life. I did not give room for any complacency or thoughts of doubt. I only listened to the Spirit and moved in accordance with His anointing. I cannot tell you how many times I have been in services when even the leaders of the house are afraid to move in prophetic or a healing anointing even when there is no doubt that the Lord is very present and imminent in the service and through the altar call.

Churches today cast doubt and dispersions on the very promises laid forth in the prophetic anointing, the Law of Moses, the covenants, and the Word of God. In Matthew 9:20-21, *"And behold, a woman who had been suffering from a hemorrhage for twelve years, came up behind Him and touched the fringe of His cloak; for she was saying to herself, "If I only touch His garment, I shall get well."* There was absolutely no doubt in this woman's mind. She had complete faith in the promises God had covenanted with to her people. She knew the Word of God and the Law of Moses. She also knew what the priestly garments worn by rabbis were representative of concerning the covenantal agreement between God and Israel.

"If you will give earnest heed to the voice of the Lord your God, and do what is right in His sight, and give ear to His commandments, and keep all His statutes, I will put none of the diseases on you which I have put on the Egyptians; for I, the Lord, am your healer" Exodus 15:26. The woman with the issue of blood knew the agreement God promised to uphold and Jesus walking in the fullness of the Spirit was not going to allow this to go unresolved. Jesus would command the healing based on the agreement He made with the nation of Israel. Within the hour she was healed after twelve years of suffering.

So why did she touch the hem of His cloak rather than speak directly to Him or to grab Him by the arm or instruct one of His disciples to relay her request? She knew the priestly garments had four tassels hanging on the cloak and what they meant. One tassel attached at each corner of the robe. The tassels were representative of the Word of God. In each tassel was a deep blue thread that represented the Law of Moses reminding Israel that they swore to obey the law. There were four tassels representing the Earth. In other words, God's Word is for all the world. In biblical numerology four is the number for Earth. The terra firma (Earth) was created on the fourth day. This woman knew that Jesus would know exactly what she was saying without uttering a word from her lips if she touched one of the tassels on the hem of His cloak. Jesus would by Exodus 15:26 fulfill God's word to her and honor His promise to be he healer. And so, she was healed.

Such great faith and complete understanding of who she is in the Kingdom of God. She knew full well that God was not going to ignore His promise to be a healer to the people of the nation of Israel. Yet, by the Holy Spirit and the act of Pentecost we carry a more powerful anointing to do the works of Christ and greater things by His testimony. So why isn't everyone who walks into church or who asks for healing healed? This is one of the greatest dilemmas in the history of Christendom. In order to justify the lack of faith in us or the lack of miraculous healings in the church we have built entire doctrinal theologies around why people do not get healed, delivered, set free, or any other encumbrance that keeps them from the visitation of God in their lives.

The church lacks the understanding of the power of confession. We have allowed cultic practices build financial empires around this very Christian principle; that God is our healer. We have books, television programs, CD's, and tapes on the best seller list reaping millions of dollars like *'The Power of Positive Thinking.'* The internet has taken over our ability to convey that healing power sits with the Christian church through the anointing of the Holy Spirit of Promise to fulfill God's word from Exodus 15:26. He is our healer.

Rationalization and Intellectual Thought

   "Professing to be wise, they became fools" Romans 1:22. And, *"For the word of **the cross** is to those who are perishing foolishness, but to us who are being saved it is **the power of God**"* 1 Corinthians 1:18.
   The cross is the power of God! So, we need to bring everything to Him and set it at the foot of power; the cross. At the cross is where we first see the light of salvation, it is the place of sacrifice, it is an altar to the heavens, and a justifier of our sinful lives. Think of that old time Gospel tune **'There is power in the Blood.'** It tells us **'there is power, power, wonder working power in the precious blood of the Lamb.'** Our inheritance is power. Our inheritance is a supernatural wonder working fulfillment of the resurrected power of Jesus Christ. There should never be any doubt in us about what God will do for us. Make your desires known to Him and verbalize the vision and gifting in your life because there is power in confession by virtue of our covenant agreement and the fulfilled Law of Moses in the cross and resurrection of Jesus Christ. We already walk in the power of that confession sealed in the Holy Spirit of Promise!
   Ministries today are in the business of rationalization when it comes to the supernatural power of God. If they cannot explain it scientifically, educationally, or theologically then it is not for their congregants. Rather than setting the example of the demonstrated power of God's Word many

ministries are intellectually setting aside its supernatural understanding. Our faith has been displaced and given over to a reprobate mind. We have allowed the science community to become the new Holy Spirit. We are changing our theology and compromising God's word and promises in order to meet scientific standards and pass muster with the intellectual community. A community that has no power to save men's souls. We cannot ignore God's precepts, doubt His promises, deny His prophetic words and still believe we can step into His greatness or have power through confessing His promises.

Some international ministries today would never use Romans 10:9-10 as a prayer for confession unto salvation because it means the participant would have to admit they were a sinner saved by grace. Sin is rarely ever spoken about in the mainline denominational churches today and a growing number of televangelists will not speak of sin because viewers will stop giving the so needed finances to keep their empires afloat.

The results of confession

It is essential that Christians make confession a daily ritual in their walks with the Lord. It is not that He needs reminding of His promises or prophetic words. He will honor the everlasting covenant that Jesus Christ secured through His ultimate sacrifice. Instead it is because confession releases the power of the supernatural and it sets things in motion.

- Confession builds relationship
- Confession releases God's power
- Confession secures our salvation
- Confession fulfills our hearing, and in our hearing, it declares the Word of God.

10

When Liberty Sets In-
Embracing a New Purpose

"If therefore the Son shall make you free, you shall be free indeed" John 8:36.

Our liberty begins in setting foundational building blocks of truth concerning the world around us. We learn that in this imperfect world we cannot expect things naturally to conform to our expectations. Our understanding that God can take what is hurtful and damaging to our emotions and turn it into our good. We also learn that our strength can function better when we let God work through our weaknesses.

In Romans 8 Paul expounds on God's principles of deliverance from bondage. The main theme of Romans 8 is to show us that God is active in the world and He has a purpose for everyone. He is sovereign over what happens to us, and He works for our good. The whole world is under tension and groans for release. Our bodies yearn and wait for the redemption which the Holy Spirit will give.

"For we know that the whole creation groans and suffers the pains of childbirth together until now. And not only this, but also, we ourselves, having the first fruits of the Spirit, even we ourselves groan within ourselves, waiting eagerly for our adoption as sons, the redemption of our body" Romans 8:22-23.

Meanwhile the Spirit helps us in our weaknesses and infirmities. *"In the same way the Spirit also helps our weakness; for we do not know how to pray as we should, but the Spirit Himself intercedes for us with groanings too deep for words"* Romans 8:26.

The healing process is a 'recycling" process in which God's grace restores people who are broken. The reality of the world is such that we cannot expect utopia. We must often settle for God's permissive will rather than His perfect will. The Lord's answer to this world's injustices and problems is the Holy Spirit whom He sent to dwell within us. The Holy Spirit is the One who stands by our side as a Helper and a Guide. *"And I will ask the Father, and He will give you another Helper, that He may be with you forever"* John 14:16. God's Holy Spirit is the third person of the Godhead who understands, who sees we are carrying a burden too heavy for us, who realizes we cannot make it on our own, who comes alongside and takes hold of the heavy burden and its pain and helps us to lift it, while enabling us to carry our crippling infirmities.

The key to understanding the grace of God is to realize that God works in and through our circumstances for our good. This is the greatest part of the healing process, that He can change hurtful insights to helpful outreach. God is not the Author of all events, but He is the Lord and Master of all events. Sin interrupts God's purposes but does not totally thwart them. It is a condition that now exists, and we must live with it realistically.

The Fall of Man through Adam caused the emotional distress and dysfunction of low self-esteem in humanity. Jesus reversed that dysfunction through His work on the cross. It was not a remaking of mankind that God set this straight but rather using the existing framework of man, He rebirthed the image of His Son into our lives through the Holy Spirit. Our reversed dysfunction lies in our surrendering to Him and becoming Christlike through His Holy Spirit. Since we are made in God's image, suffering from Adam's fall, yearns for the wholeness and unity with God that will give complete peace and rest. It is in our Oneness with Jesus through Holy Spirit that we are eternally connected to the Father. *"If you had known Me, you would have known My Father also; from now on you know Him and have seen Him"* John 15:7.

This is a marvelous revelation! What a picture of healing and wholeness! We are in Oneness with the Father through the work of Jesus Christ. Walking in Oneness with God is the key to healing for our damaged emotions. The more we become like Him by His Holy Spirit, the more the dysfunctional emotions of the flesh begin to fade. We can never in this life walk in complete emotional healing, but we can control the effects and the outcome of our emotions by realizing by His Spirit we are **more than conquerors**. Our understanding is enlightened giving us control over the flesh so as not to react from a damaged state but rather to respond in spiritual maturity.

We need to acknowledge the reality of sin and its power in the world. If we deny sin or minimize its significance, we have created a dream world built on a faulty foundation of sand. It cannot stand the test of time when the rain, wind, and floods of life come against us. We never get to the root of the problem; our attempts to envision utopia cloud our vision of the real world.

We need to understand the importance of the biblical view of Creation, the Fall, and redemption. If we see the whole of God's plan as it is, we get a better picture of the present world.

The Holy Spirit has a significant place in healing our emotions. Romans 8:26 speaks to our weaknesses, in the Greek this is better interpreted as infirmities. We have infirmities [weaknesses] in us that are not necessarily related to sin. V26 describes the role of the Holy Spirit as a Helper [*Paraclete*}. There is a significant difference in the spiritual reality of the Holy Spirit's role. He is the One who intercedes for us and not we ourselves from our own strength [systems of works] stemming from the lie that we are only as good as what we do. By the Holy Spirit we are good because Jesus died for us. God sees our righteous through the work of Jesus Christ sealed in the Holy Spirit of Promise. This understanding defeats the precepts put forth in us through a perfectionism. We are perfect because of Christ not because of what we do. **This is a liberating statement!** Practice it, walk in it, get it into your Spirit, and make it a daily prayer in your life.

Romans 8:27 speaks to intercession by the Holy Spirit according to the perfect will of God concerning us [the saints]. *"And He who searches the hearts knows what the mind of the Spirit is, because He intercedes for the saints according to the will of God."* The implication relates to the deeper inner self, the great storehouse of our memories where our hurts and pains lie buried too deep for ordinary prayer, sometimes too deep for an audible prayer—this is where emotional healing takes place by the work of the Holy Spirit.

"Down in the human heart, crushed by the tempter,
Feelings lie buried that grace can restore:
Touched by a loving heart, wakened by kindness,
Chords that are broken will vibrate once more."
"Rescue the Perishing" — Fanny Crosby

If you know little of Fanny Crosby's life these words reflect tremendous insight into God's love and tenderness to her. She knew the actions of God's grace in her own life during her 95 years, though she was blinded from the age of six weeks.

Romans 8:28 is often quoted out of context. There is a big difference between saying that **all things work** together for our good, or that God **in all things works** for our good. The second is the preferred interpretation [in all things works]. What is the real promise of God in Romans 8:28? God is not the Author of all events, but He is the Lord and Master of all events. No matter what we do, we can rest assured through the working power of the cross of Jesus Christ and the intercession of the Holy Spirit on our behalf that we will receive good from God.

There is a distinction between the _event_ of what happens and the _meaning_ of what happens. The event of what happens places its emphasis on ALL THINGS; "*All things work together for good.*" In this interpretive definition God in not the Author of all things. Now consider the interpretive definition where God is Lord and Master of all things. The meaning of what happens places its emphasis on GOOD; "*In all things God works for good.*" The Lord in the latter interpretation has our best interest in mind and by His word in Romans 8:26-28 accomplishes it through the work of the Holy Spirit. The work is not ours [removal of the system of works] but rather it is His [enter a system of grace]. This is a liberating revelation!

We need help in our weaknesses. We need to admit or assert that God used man's injustice and weakness to bring about salvation through Jesus' death. Our glory rests in the cross of Jesus Christ. There are two aspects of man's glory; the cross of Jesus Christ and man's weaknesses. "*Therefore, I am well content with weaknesses, with insults, with distresses, with persecutions, with difficulties, for Christ's sake; for when I am weak, then I am strong*" 2 Corinthians 12:10.

We do not need to shrink away from our weaknesses. We need to become vulnerable to them. It is never wrong to admit fear and anxiety. There is a temptation to impress others as being wise and above the battle when fear and anxiety are at our doorstep. But when we strain to be better or super-spiritual, we often separate ourselves from others. They just don't think we understand. If we become vulnerable, as Jesus was in the Garden of Gethsemane, we show others that our strengths stem from letting the Holy Spirit help us in our own need. Others will see that as we were in the battle and have overcome, so can they.

Our challenge then, is to continue to be open to God and to those close to us, as we seek emotional expression that ever moves closer to God's purposes for all of us.

Conditions of our Liberty

Forgiveness. The spiritual act of forgiveness is one of the most critical decisions we can make in our healing process. It is God's desire that we walk in instant forgiveness, not only forgiving ourselves but forgiving those who have wronged us. The scriptural principle of forgiveness is for our benefit not for those we are forgiving. Forgiveness sets us free from debt collecting, a wrong held against others, and it gives us the freedom to move on without restraints. It is so important to the Lord that it is the only requirement in the Lord's Prayer in Matthew 6:12, "*And forgive us our sins* (the plea for mercy), *as we also have forgiven those who have sinned against us* (the condition of that plea)." If we do not forgive others, then God will not forgive us. If we harbor unforgiveness in our heart, we will be set completely free from our emotional pain. Forgiveness requires a no judgment attitude.

Reconciliation. If we are to experience true liberation from the bondage of our damaged emotions, we must be reconciled to those we have been estranged to. Not all reconciliation is reciprocal, however our efforts are required by the Lord. *'If therefore you are presenting your offering at the altar, and there remember that your brother has something against you, leave your offering there before the altar, and go your way; first be reconciled to your brother, and then come and present your offering"* Matthew 5:23-24. If you have made your reconciliation attempts known and they are not received by those you are trying to reconcile with, you are released, and God will not hold any wrong against you thereby receiving your offering at His altar.

Restoration. The conditions of restoration have brought about a turning toward the direction of God. In our emotional dysfunction, we had been walking in a direction away from the Lord. We must make a 180-degree correction in our journey and keep our compass pointed to the altar of Jesus Christ; His cross, His Spirit, increased Christlikeness. Our focus needs to be stayed on the things of God and the understanding that His love for us is the grace we so desperately need. It is a removal of the system of works that has ruled in us for so many years, even to three generations in our families. It has placed us on a path of grace and acceptance of God's love.

Embracing a New Purpose. *"And they were continually amazed at His teaching, for His message was with authority"* Luke 4:32. If you have ever been sitting in a dark place for a time, maybe indoors, then begin to open the outside door into the bright sunshine of the day, your pupils contract to protect your eyesight until an adjustment occurs. Once the adjustment takes hold you observe the beauty around you caused by the effects of the sun; flowers blooming, birds chirping, colors popping, increased senses; feeling the warmth of the sun, the light breeze brushing up against you, people interacting and enjoying the sunshine. There is an illumination of the senses. The sunshine brings happiness into people's lives. Many psychologists agree that the sunshine increases the endorphins in our brains causing us to feel happier and giving us a better disposition to face the day. A beautiful sunny day puts most people in a great frame of mind.

In the same way, when the revelation of God's Word comes alive in us, we experience life from a new perspective. The Spirit brings joy, peace, love, kindness, patience, goodness, faithfulness, gentleness, and self-control (Galatians 5:22-23) into our lives. He makes it come alive in us. Letting go of the old actions of the flesh when facing life is like walking into the sunshine from the darkness for the first time. Our soul [mind] has been set free from the bondage of a system of works and brought us into the glory of His grace [sunshine]. Walking a grace anointing has been the plan of God from the beginning of time and was implemented at the fall of man in the Garden of Eden.

The love of God for you is not based on performance but rather on His desire for an intimate relationship with you.

"...Thou art intimately acquainted with all my ways" Psalm 139:3.

Understanding this truth will place you on a new beginning of fresh revelation. It is liberating to the soul and it brings healing to the emotional damage that has kept you in bondage for many years. Our focus must be on Christlikeness in every aspect of our lives. Having a vertical approach to life is the key to your overcoming the emotional damage and the rejection you have faced. God re-builds a new foundation that is built on the rock. No matter what the enemy brings against it, the rock will stand.

Embracing a new purpose in your walk with Him opens the door to giving a new understanding of who God really is. It places Him completely in control of all situations in your life. He only wants good for you. His purpose is to complete the work of His Son in you. By embracing this revelation your ministry will increase, your preaching will be with more power, your anointing will be a constant presence of God's grace. You will understand God's will for your life.

In my book, "Stepping Into Greatness," I expound on how to set the foundations of a powerful Christian life. Embracing a new purpose is setting those foundations so that the life you are now building will be set on the solid rock of Jesus Christ. Instead of being in a constant battle of 'why doesn't anything good ever happen to me' and the negativity of that statement to speak death into your life, you are setting your mind on building the kingdom of God in you and replacing death with life; *"I can do all things through Christ who strengthens me"* Philippians 4:13. This becomes your defining statement!

A minister who had taken my counseling class on "Healing for Damaged Emotions," testified to the changing effects this course had on his life. It was a defining moment for him in his ministry. The change in him was so acute [intense] that he confessed to tossing his old teaching materials and ministry tapes because he could sense the damaged emotional issues in his preaching. He did not want that work to define who he was as a minister. He admitted that the new understanding God had given him about who he really is to God and the call God placed on his life were now more defined. His preaching changed. He admitted his congregation noticed the difference. It was more loving, more forgiving, and filled with God's grace. He testified that new doors were being opened to his ministry, doors that had been closed to him in the past. God was fulfilling the desires of his heart by increasing the venues and opportunities. He was writing books, printing and distributing teaching materials, teaching at a local Bible college, and broadcasting on Christian television. He admitted in the past, his ministry was to satisfy a self-indulgence in him. He liked the idea of ministry. Today, however, he understands his calling and God has renewed his love for the ministry. He admitted to walking in liberty for the first time in many years. He has freedom. A freedom that only Christ can give. He has become more than a conqueror!

Overcomers

The Greek word for overcomer is *'nikao.'* Its literal translation is to conquer, prevail, and get the victory. It needs to be pointed out that victors, those who prevail, have fought a war or have been in a conflict. They triumphed! When a conquering nation enters the country they defeated, they secure not only the land, its inhabitants, and the infrastructure but the GOVERNMENT! The seat of power. As an overcomer, *"...the word of God abides in you, and you have overcome the evil one"* 1 John 2:14. God has made us governors of Judah [praise] Zech. 12:6. We rule in heavenly places. We sit and reign with the King of kings and Lord of lords. We are heirs with Him and are called children of God (1 John 3:1).

"Everyone who has this hope fixed on Him purifies himself, just as He is pure" 1 John 3:3.

Governors write proclamations and make declarations. You need to declare your liberty from emotional damage.

Walk in your governmental anointing. *"You have been raised up with Christ, keep seeking the things above, where Christ is, seated at the right hand of God. Set your mind on the things above [the Spirit], not on the things that are on the earth [the flesh]'* Colossians 3:1-2. This passage speaks to putting on the new self which is Christ.

Walk in a Praise Anointing

In Zechariah 12:6, the Scripture tells us we are *"governors of Judah."* The Hebrew interpretation of Judah literally means praise. God is prophesying to us that we are governors [leaders who sit in governmental power] of praise. Praise gives us authority [governors].

When Christians think of making a difference in the world our attention is immediately turned to missions, outreach, prayer, or other acts of service. Although these ministries are important to the kingdom of God, the Lord is raising an army of people who are call **"Governors of Praise."** *"I will make the governors of Judah [praise] like a firepan in the woodpile, and like a fiery torch in the sheaves; they shall devour all the surrounding peoples [enemies]...but Jerusalem shall be inhabited again"* Zechariah 12:6

When the Bible refers to a fiery torch, it is speaking about the lightning that surrounds the throne of God (Rev. 4:5). The word "peoples" in Zechariah means nations. It is important to understand that things happen around the throne of God. Destinies are released, promises are fulfilled, assignments are commanded, and territories are taken for the kingdom of God.

We must take on a governing role in our praise. Our praise should not just be words mouthed from a defeated position on earth. Our praise is destined to take up a position of victory from in the heavens. I do NOT prophesy into lives to take a position against something that is over you. But to help you take a prophetic seat as judge and governor in the heavens over your situation. We speak against the forces of darkness and place that evil beneath our feet. *"The last enemy...destroyed is death. For He has put all things* [enemies-emotional damage-poverty-sickness-and the like] *under our feet"* 1 Corinthians 15:26-27.

When you become a governor of praise, God begins to crush Satan under your feet and you begin to walk in victory!

There is a common misunderstanding about praise. Praising God helps to strengthen our spirits. This is true, however not all praise and worship do this. In Psalm 8:2, *"Out of the mouths of babes and nursing infants you have ordained strength* [NIV translation is praise}, *because of your enemies, that you may silence the enemy and the avenger."* Jesus proclaimed in Matthew 21:16, *"...have you never read, that out of the mouths of babes and nursing infants you have perfected praise."* When you praise God you receive strength; when we examine Psalm 8:2 further, we should ask the question, God has ordained praise for what reason? The answer is clear. Because of the enemies of the Lord.

God has ordained praise so that we can overcome our enemy. In other words, God ordained praise so that we will SHUT THE DEVIL UP! Do you want to shut the devil up and keep his voice out of your life? Then praise and worship the Lord. This is governmental praise. Taking your rightful seat with Christ in heavenly places.

Praising God does not include, "Oh Lord, I beg of you...or God I don't know it you are going to fulfill your promise to me...or I just don't know it its your will." NOT AT ALL!

Effective praise knows the will of the Father, and it speaks forth that will into the earth. When true praise goes forth, it silences the enemy. You have overcome them because He has overcome the world (1 John 4:4). This understanding will lead you into the confidence that all of God's plans for you are good not evil. And when you are governing your life and the assigned territory around you with praise, His will and His good plans will come to pass.

A Firepan and a Fiery Torch

"Like a firepan in the woodpile, and like a fiery torch in the sheaves they shall devour the nations..." Zechariah 12:6. In many churches praise and worship is lukewarm at best. It's weak and the devil has taken residence there. We have allowed our praise and worship in some churches to become so 'user-friendly' that it becomes unfriendly to God. Worship is not about us — it's all about God. We need to become Holy Spirit sensitive when it comes to praise and worship.

Psalm 68:1, *"Let God arise, and His enemies be scattered."* When we are a church where God is arising amid His people, His enemies scatter. They can't dwell in His presence. Sickness, low self-esteem, damaged emotions, disease, depression, and any other worldly distraction cannot dwell amid a governor's praise. When someone with cancer or any other type of disease enters, the disease can't stay because the presence of God overwhelms the adversary.

In Hebrew, a firepan is a platform. The governors of praise are to be a platform making declarations of praise to God. Governors make declarations and proclamations.

A fiery torch in Hebrew is defined, "to shine." When governors of praise proclaim praises unto Him, He decrees and declares victory and it silences the enemy in our region.

Our praise is not for us alone or the just the house of God, but it is designed to go forth into the atmosphere effectively changing the spiritual environment of our region and the nations of the world.

Are you ready to see something catch fire and begin to burn inside of you? God is looking for a people who will return to the state of burning passion for Him, for His house, and for praise.

In the Sheaves

Zechariah 12:6 tells us the torch is to be lit "in the sheaves." The Hebrew interpretation of the sheaves is a handful. It is speaking to the feast of Tabernacles and the last great harvest. God desires the sheaves to be wrapped around you and set aflame for Him. God is raising a people on fire for Him and who will release Heaven on Earth. God wants the fire He places in us so hot that it can't be handled. It will administer the ushering in of the Harvest and be so hot that the forces of darkness will not be able to hold it.

Final thoughts

Our victory rests in our desire to be more Christlike. It is accepting the truth of God's word that He only administers good into our lives. Do not let your past dictate your future. *"Finally, brethren, whatever is true, whatever is honorable, whatever is right, whatever is pure, whatever is lovely, whatever is of good repute, if there is any excellence and if anything is worthy of praise, let your mind dwell on these things"* Philippians 4:8.

BIBLIOGRAPHY

New American Standard Bible, Holman Publishers, Nashville, TN

Stepping Into Greatness, Dr. Steve Rocco, Calvary Int'l Publishing Co., Cromwell, CT 06416

The New Strong's Concise Concordance, Thomas Nelson Publishers, Nashville, TN

Healing for Damaged Emotions, Dr. David Seamands, Victor Books

The Lies We Believe, Dr. Chris Thurman, Thomas Nelson Publishers, Nashville, TN

Dake's Annotated Reference Bible, Dake Publishing, Inc., Lawrenceville, GA 30046

Getting the Best of Your Anger, Les Carter, Baker House Publishing Group, Grand Rapids, MI 49516-6287

Married Without Masks, Nancy Groom, NavPress, Colorado Springs, CO 80934

The Fantasy Fallacy, Shannon Etheridge, Thomas Nelson Publishers, Nashville, TN

Building Your Mate's Self-esteem, Dennis & Barbara Rainey, Here's Life Publishers, San Bernardino, CA 92402

Reconcilable Differences, Jim Talley, Thomas Nelson Publishers, Nashville, TN

Made in the USA
Middletown, DE
02 December 2018